Active Transportation and Real Estate

THE NEXT FRONTIER

Urban Land Institute

Building Healthy
Places Initiative

Cover: The Schuylkill Banks Boardwalk forms a key section of the Circuit regional trail network, a burgeoning 750-mile (1,200 km) collection of trails that connects people and places throughout Greater Philadelphia and southern New Jersey. Nearby developments have leveraged access to the trail as a key differentiating amenity and have accommodated bicycle use within buildings. *(© Richard Nowitz/Getty Images)*

Recommended bibliographic listing:
Urban Land Institute: *Active Transportation and Real Estate: The Next Frontier.* Washington, D.C.: the Urban Land Institute, 2016.

ISBN: 978-0-87420-362-2

About the Urban Land Institute

The Urban Land Institute is a nonprofit research and education organization whose mission is to provide leadership in the responsible use of land and in creating and sustaining thriving communities worldwide. Established in 1936, the Institute today has more than 37,000 members and associates from 82 countries, representing the entire spectrum of the land use and development disciplines.

ULI relies heavily on the experience of its members. It is through member involvement and information resources that ULI has been able to set standards of excellence in development practice. The Institute is recognized internationally as one of America's most respected and widely quoted sources of objective information on urban planning, growth, and development.

About the Building Healthy Places Initiative

Around the world, communities face pressing health challenges related to the built environment. Through the Building Healthy Places Initiative, launched in summer 2013, ULI is leveraging the power of ULI's global networks to shape projects and places in ways that improve the health of people and communities. Learn more and connect with Building Healthy Places: http://www.uli.org/health. Share your story via Twitter: #ulihealth.

About This Report

Active Transportation and Real Estate: The Next Frontier explores the interconnections among walking, bicycling, and real estate. Developers, owners, property managers, designers, investors, public officials, and others involved in real estate decision making can learn from the case studies described in this report to create places that both support and leverage investments in active transportation infrastructure, such as bike lanes and trails. In the process, they can create real estate value and promote economic, environmental, and public health goals.

ULI is grateful to the **Colorado Health Foundation** for its support of this project and the Building Healthy Places Initiative, as well as to the Randall Lewis Health Policy Fellowship Program for its assistance with research.

Contents

CHAPTER 1

Trends in Active Transportation

Active transportation was, until recently, the forgotten mode of travel. However, in recent years, investments in infrastructure that accommodates those who walk and ride bicycles have begun to reshape communities. Sometimes called "nonmotorized transportation," active transportation involves human-powered activity, primarily walking and bicycling.

Walking, of course, is as old as humankind, but in places around the world, including the United States—a country that over the past several decades has been designed around motor vehicles—walking and bicycling came to be considered the domain of children, the elderly, or people without the financial means to own a car. Today, however, walkable and bike-friendly communities are growing in popularity.

Fifty percent of U.S. residents say that walkability is a top priority or a high priority when considering where to live, according to the Urban Land Institute's *America in 2015* report, and, according to the U.S. Census, bicycling has become the country's fastest-growing form of transportation for commuters.

Bike-sharing systems are becoming increasingly popular in cities throughout the world. *(Shutterstock/Rostislav Glinsky)*

Bicycling is also still growing in popularity in places that started making the shift to bicycle transportation over the last half-century. The city of Amsterdam, for instance, reports that even though it has long been known as one of the most bike-friendly cities in the world, the number of local bicycle trips has increased by more than 40 percent since the 1990s.

Other world capitals, such as Singapore, currently have comparatively low bicycling rates, but are investing in infrastructure to promote cycling as a healthy, environmentally friendly commuting option. In 2011, only 1 percent of all trips in Singapore were by bicycle, but the government aims to significantly increase this figure by creating safer and more convenient bike routes.

Communities big and small are now investing in bicycle and pedestrian infrastructure. These trends are reshaping destinations across the globe, and have the potential to benefit people of all income brackets, since biking provides mobility for those needing or wanting a less expensive alternative to automobile ownership, maintenance, and use. This report examines the implications of the growing interest in active transportation on economic development, public health, air quality, community design, and real estate investment.

Research shows that the built environment (including buildings, streets, and neighborhoods) has a profound impact on health outcomes. An *American Journal of Preventative Medicine* study found that people who live in neighborhoods with shops and retail establishments within walking distance have a 35 percent lower risk of obesity.

Bicycling can also reduce energy consumption and greenhouse gas emissions. The European Cyclists Federation found that, if levels of cycling in the European Union were equivalent to those found in Denmark, where the average person cycles almost 600 miles (965 km) each year, bicycle use alone would achieve 26 percent of the 2050 greenhouse gas reduction targets set for the transportation sector.

Integrating bike-friendly infrastructure into development projects allows cyclists to make active transportation a part of their daily lives. *(Ed McMahon)*

Through supporting bike infrastructure, real estate professionals who influence the built environment can play a significant role in creating healthier, more sustainable communities. They can also help position their projects and communities in a marketplace that increasingly values active transportation.

Bicycling Is Booming

Bicycling has recently undergone a renaissance in locations across the world, with an increasing number of people taking to the streets by bike. In the United States, the U.S. Census showed that the number of people who traveled to work by bike increased roughly 62 percent between 2000 and 2014, while Transport for London found that, in 2014, cycling in London reached its highest rate since record keeping began.

Economic considerations, such as the high cost of owning, operating, and insuring a car—which averaged nearly $8,700 in the United States in 2015, according to AAA—as well as environmental, social, and health factors, have caused a boom in the cycling economy, with indications that this will be a long-term trend.

Who is biking and why? The answer is all kinds of people, on all kinds of bikes, for all kinds of reasons. Today, one sees kids biking to soccer practice, men and women in business attire headed to work, people making short trips to the grocery store or to visit friends, college students going to class, senior citizens out for exercise, and tour groups on bicycle vacations.

It is generally only when cities invest in bicycle infrastructure that residents and visitors begin to use bicycles at rates that exceed the national average. Consider Portland, Oregon, for example: In the 1980s and early 1990s, Portland was a city pretty much like any other in terms of transportation behavior. As of 2014, more than 7 percent of residents commuted to work by bicycle, compared with the national average of less than 1 percent (see figure 1).

Bicycle use in Portland has grown exponentially while other modes have grown relatively modestly or declined. According to the City of Portland Bureau of Transportation, bicycle commuting since 1990 has grown by 400 percent, while transit has grown by just 18 percent and driving has declined by 4 percent.

Steve Towsen, Portland's city engineer, attributes the bicycling boom to investment in bicycle infrastructure, saying, "Bicycling infrastructure is relatively easy to implement and low-cost compared to other modes."

The city of Portland estimated the cost of its 300-mile (483 km) network of bike trails, bike lanes, and bike boulevards at approximately $60 million in 2008, which is about the same cost as one mile (1.6 km) of four-lane urban freeway.

Another city where bicycling has boomed is Minneapolis. According to the U.S. Census, almost 5 percent of Minneapolis residents biked to work in 2014, and bike commuting grew by more than 186 percent between 1990 and 2014.

Even in winter, approximately one-third of regular commuters bike to work at least some of the time, according to Bike Walk Twin Cities. As of 2015, Minneapolis had 129 miles (208 km) of on-street bikeways and 97 miles (156 km) of off-street bikeways, with plans to keep growing the network. "Biking is a huge part of who we are," explains R.T. Ryback, former mayor of Minneapolis.

Minneapolis has a long-term goal of 15 percent of citywide transportation being by bicycle by 2025. This is certainly possible if one considers that several large European cities—such as Copenhagen and Amsterdam—have bicycle commuting rates exceeding 40 percent, according to Copenhagenize, an international bike and pedestrian consultant firm. According to the U.S. Department of Transportation's 2009 National Household Travel Survey, half of all trips taken by people in the United States are under three miles (equivalent to a 20-minute bike ride). This shows that Minneapolis's goal could be achieved with continuing investments in bicycling infrastructure. Bicycle commuting rates are also growing in the largest U.S. cities (places with populations exceeding 1 million). The U.S. Census showed that Philadelphia had the highest bicycle commuting rate in 2014, at 1.9 percent, followed by Chicago at 1.7 percent. Philadelphia's bike commuting rate grew nearly 237 percent between 1990 and 2014, and the rate in Chicago grew at a whopping 506 percent during the same period.

FIGURE 1
Bicycle Commuting Rate for Large U.S. Cities, 2014

City	Rate
Portland, OR	7.2%
Minneapolis, MN	4.7%
San Francisco, CA	4.4%
Washington, DC	3.9%
Seattle, WA	3.7%
Oakland, CA	3.7%
Tucson, AZ	3.5%
New Orleans, LA	3.4%
Denver, CO	2.5%
Boston, MA	2.4%

Source: U.S. Census Bureau, American Community Survey 2014, Journey to Work.

Economic Benefits of Active Transportation

As bicycling and walking networks have grown, so have active transportation–oriented developments and bike-friendly businesses. The bicycle industry sold over $6 billion worth of bikes and equipment in 2014, according to the National Bicycle Dealers Association.

A 1996 American Greenways Program study found that the Denver metropolitan area (population at the time, about 2 million) had 149 bicycle dealers. By contrast, the Atlanta metropolitan area, with a population of more than 3 million, had only 28 bicycle dealers. The explanation: In 1996, Denver had 200 miles (322 km) of paved off-road bike trails, while the Atlanta area had fewer than

Four Ways Protected Bike Lanes Boost Economic Growth

 Fueling redevelopment to boost real estate value. As city populations grow, motor vehicle congestion increases. New roads are rarely an option in mature cities. Protected bike lanes bring order and predictability to streets and provide transportation choices while helping build neighborhoods where everyone enjoys spending time. By extending the geographic range of travel, bike lanes help neighborhoods redevelop without waiting years for new transit service to debut.

 Making workers healthier and more productive. From D.C. to Chicago to Portland, the story is the same: people go out of their way to use protected bike lanes. By creating clear delineation between auto and bike traffic, protected bike lanes get more people in the saddle—burning calories, clearing minds, and strengthening hearts and lungs. As companies scramble to lower health care costs, employees who benefit from the gentle exercise of pedaling to work help boost overall hourly productivity and cut bills.

 Helping companies score talented workers. Savvy workers, especially millennials and members of generation X, increasingly prefer downtown jobs and nearby homes. Because protected bike lanes make biking more comfortable and popular, they help companies locate downtown without breaking the bank on auto parking space, and allow workers to reach their desk the way they increasingly prefer: under their own power.

 Increasing retail visibility and sales volume. In growing urban communities, protected bike lane networks encourage more people to ride bikes for everyday trips. And when people use bikes for errands, they are the ideal kind of retail customers: regulars. They stop by often and spend as much or more per month as people who arrive in cars. Plus, ten customers who arrive by bike fit in the parking space of one customer who arrives by car.

Source: Text verbatim from "Protected Bike Lanes Mean Business," by PeopleforBikes and the Alliance for Biking & Walking.

20 miles (32 km). Since that time, the Atlanta region, with the help of local cycling advocates and federal transportation monies, has built numerous bike trails and is advancing a bicycle beltway, which is known as the Atlanta BeltLine.

The economic impact of bicycling and walking goes well beyond bike sales. Numerous studies have shown that real estate values increase with proximity to bicycle paths and walking trails. For example:

>> **Indianapolis, Indiana.** A 2014 study of Indianapolis's eight-mile (13 km) Indianapolis Cultural Trail by the Indiana University Public Policy Institute found that since its opening in 2008, the value of properties within a block of this high-quality biking and walking trail has risen an astonishing 148 percent. The value of the nearly 1,800 parcels within 500 feet (152 m) of the trail increased by more than $1.01 billion over the same period. Given the fact that this eight-mile (13 km) landscaped trail around the heart of the city cost only $62.5 million (mostly provided by private or philanthropic sources, as well as a federal Transportation Investment Generating Economic Recovery [TIGER] grant), the city has declared it not just a quality-of-life asset, but an economic boon as well.

>> **Dallas, Texas.** Since the opening of the 3.5-mile (5.6 km) Katy Trail in the Uptown neighborhood of Dallas in 2006, property values have climbed nearly 80 percent, to $3.4 billion, according to Uptown's business improvement district.

>> **Radnor, Pennsylvania.** A 2011 study by the GreenSpace Alliance and the Delaware Valley Regional Planning Commission found that properties within a quarter-mile (0.4 km) of the Radnor Trail in Radnor Township, Pennsylvania, were valued on average $69,139 higher than other area properties further away. Real estate listings in Radnor frequently mention trail access in their advertisements.

- >> **Atlanta BeltLine.** In 2013, REMAX Realty in Atlanta explained that homes near the BeltLine—a transit and trail loop around the city that will include a planned total of 33 miles (53 km) of pedestrian and bicycle trails—were selling within 24 hours. Before the Atlanta BeltLine project began, homes along the corridor had typically stayed on the market for 60 to 90 days.
- >> **Minneapolis, Minnesota.** A University of Minnesota study found that, in the Minneapolis/St. Paul area, for every 1,312 feet (400 m) closer a median-priced home is to an off-street bicycle facility, its value increases by $510.
- >> **United States.** A 2009 nationwide study by CEOs for Cities, a cross-sector organization that develops ideas to make U.S. cities more economically successful, found that "houses located in areas with above-average walkability or bikability are worth up to $34,000 more than similar houses in areas with average walkability levels."

Bike lanes physically separated from the roadway provide safe ways to integrate cycling as part of a city's transportation system. *(Shutterstock/Ashira Maythamongkhonkhet)*

ACTIVE TRANSPORTATION, RETAIL, AND ECONOMIC DEVELOPMENT

A growing body of evidence exists that bicycling has a positive impact on retail sales, commercial property values, and overall economic development. In fact, a growing group of entrepreneurial innovators are discovering that bike trails and bike lanes can help modern retailers get more customers in the door and boost sales. In Europe and Asia, bikes have long been used for shopping and other everyday errands. Now, Americans are learning that bikes equipped with baskets or racks can make shopping fun and easy.

Research by the Alliance for Bicycling and Walking shows that customers who bike to a store typically buy less in a single visit than people who drive, but they return more often and spend more overall per month.

Some examples of the positive impact of cycling on retail sales and on commercial and economic development include the following:

- >> **New York, New York.** A 2011 study by the New York City Department of Transportation found that rents along New York City's Times Square pedestrian areas and bicycle lanes increased 71 percent in 2010. This was the greatest rise in the city and a sign that there is a high demand for and low supply of human-friendly streets.
- >> **Salt Lake City, Utah.** A study by the Salt Lake City Department of Transportation found that "replacing parking with protected bike lanes increased retail sales." A general street upgrade on Broadway Avenue removed 30 percent of on-street parking from nine blocks of the major commercial street, but improved crosswalks and sidewalks and added protected bike lanes. In the first six months of the next year, retail sales were up 8.8 percent over the first six months of the previous year, compared with a citywide increase of only 7 percent. After the changes, 59 percent of business owners said they supported the street improvements, while only 18 percent opposed them.
- >> **Dunedin, Florida.** A study of the Pinellas Trail found that retail vacancies in the town of Dunedin, Florida, declined by more than 50 percent after the opening of the popular trail. New businesses included several restaurants, a bike shop, an outdoor equipment supplier, a bed-and-breakfast operation, and a coffee shop.

FIGURE 2

Shopping by Bicycle Leads to Smaller Trips and More Visits

People who arrive to a business on a bike spend less per visit but visit more often than people who arrive by car, resulting in more money spent overall per month.

Source: "Protected Bike Lanes Mean Business," PeopleForBikes and the Alliance for Biking & Walking.

>> **San Francisco, California.** A San Francisco State University study found that when the city of San Francisco reduced car lanes and installed bike lanes and wider sidewalks on Valencia Street, two-thirds of merchants said the increased levels of bicycling and walking improved business. Only 4 percent said the changes hurt sales.

>> **Sydney, Australia.** The city of Sydney found that building 124 miles (200 km) of planned bikeways would generate at least AU$506 million (US$354 million) in economic benefits. The network was also expected to reduce traffic congestion by 4.3 million car trips per year and to increase bicycle trips by 66 percent by 2016, leading to AU$147 million (US$103 million) in additional health benefits.

>> **United Kingdom.** The London School of Economics found in 2011 that cycling generates nearly £3 billion (US$4.32 billion) for the United Kingdom's economy each year.

BICYCLING AND TOURISM

Bike-friendly cities and towns are also finding that bicycle facilities boost the tourism economy and encourage extended stays and return visits. Tourism is one of the world's largest industries. The U.S. Travel Association explains that U.S. residents spend over $800 billion a year on travel and recreation away from home.

Bike touring and recreational bicycling have long been staples of the tourism economy. In Wisconsin, for example, bike tourism is estimated to contribute $1.5 billion to the state's economy each year, according to a University of Wisconsin–Madison study. Bicycle-friendly communities are finding that bike trails and other active transportation infrastructure encourage visitors to stay longer, spend more, and come back more often.

More people ride bikes than play golf or ski. Bicycle-friendly destinations like Sanibel Island, Florida; St. Simon's Island, Georgia; and Hilton Head, South Carolina, have long known that bike trails and walking paths are very good for tourism and for second-home development. Charles Fraser, the developer of Sea Pines Resort on Hilton Head Island, South Carolina's first master-planned community, often told friends that many more people came to walk and ride bikes on the resort's trails and beaches than came to play golf. *Hilton Head Magazine* explains that the success of the 15 miles (24 km) of paved trails in Sea Pines eventually led to the creation of a total of 112 miles (180 km) of trails across Hilton Head Island and that demand for bike rentals within the resort went up by more than 25 percent between 2011 and 2014.

Top: Scenic pathways can connect bicyclists with nature and recreational destinations as well as with urban centers. *(Shutterstock/HeliHead)*

Bottom: Bicycling is one of the most popular forms of transportation in Amsterdam, where there are more bikes than residents. *(Shutterstock/kavram)*

What's more, bicycle infrastructure can help tourism-oriented communities maximize the benefits of tourism while minimizing burdens such as traffic congestion. Bike-friendly destinations, like Nantucket and Martha's Vineyard in Massachusetts, have reduced the need for large, unsightly, and expensive motor vehicle parking lots by constructing a network of off-road bike paths that provide easy access to island beaches and other attractions. A North Carolina Department of Transportation study found that a one-time investment of $6.7 million for a network of bike lanes in the Outer Banks has yielded an annual nine-to-one return on investment thanks to increased bicycle tourism.

Bike races and bike touring are another part of the growing bicycle economy. Consider, for instance, RAGBRAI, which stands for "the Register's Annual Great Bicycle Ride Across Iowa." Now in its 44th year, this seven-day event attracts tens of thousands of participants who cycle across Iowa following a different route each year. The ride has a huge economic impact for the state— a 2008 study by the University of Northern Iowa found that the event generates over $25 million in direct spending. The small towns along the route compete to provide lodging and sell food, beer, massages, souvenirs, and much more to the thousands of participants and spectators who take part each year.

Likewise, in 2014, the first stages of the Tour de France bicycle race took place in the United Kingdom. A study by event organizers, including Leeds City Council and Transport for London, found that this "Grand Départ" generated £128 million (US$184 million) in total revenue, with £102 million (US$146 million) for the Yorkshire region alone.

In addition to large bicycle events, individual and small-group bike touring is growing by leaps and bounds. A 2012 European Union study found that an estimated 2.3 billion cycle tourism trips occur in Europe, with a value greater than €44 billion (US$48 billion) per year.

In the Canadian province of Quebec, a 2014 study by the University of Quebec at Montreal found that cycling tourists spend an average CAD$214 (US$152) per day—6 percent more than other types of tourists while cycling the La Route Verte, a 3,128-mile (5,034 km) bikeway network in Quebec.

In the United States, a 2012 study of the Great Allegheny Passage trail in Pennsylvania and Maryland found that businesses along the trail attribute 30 percent of their gross revenues to the trail, and close to half of the surveyed businesses said that the trail was a significant factor in their decisions to expand.

Bicycle Infrastructure

Bicycle use, whether for transportation or recreation, is highly dependent on the existence of bicycle infrastructure. Experience demonstrates that investments in bicycle infrastructure yield results regardless of climate, topography, city size, or other factors. The biggest impediment to more widespread bicycle use is people's fear of being hit by a motor vehicle. Steady increases in bicycling can be traced to increases in the safety and convenience of bicycle infrastructure. As recently as 25 years ago in the United States, just about the only place to ride a bike was in the street, where riders had to compete with drivers.

Then, in 1991, the U.S. Congress passed the Intermodal Surface Transportation Efficiency Act (ISTEA), which for the first time set aside federal transportation dollars for the construction of bicycle and pedestrian infrastructure. While less than 2 percent of federal transportation funding went into bicycling and pedestrian projects, this amounted to a huge increase in funding for bicycle infrastructure.

According to the Federal Highway Administration, in 1992, only 50 bike projects received federal funding. By 2002, the number of bike projects receiving federal funding had jumped to 1,287; and by 2010, the federal government was funding 2,763 projects.

No longer relying solely on traditional bike lanes with just a few inches of white paint to give people on bikes a feeling of safety on busy city streets, modern bikeway design includes grade-separated bike trails, protected bike lanes (bike lanes using curbs, planters, parked cars, or simple posts to clearly separate bikes from auto traffic and sidewalks), and bicycle boulevards (low-traffic streets optimized for cycling). Now there are even so-called bicycle freeways that include separate unidirectional paths for each direction of bicycle travel that are fully segregated from pedestrian paths.

A 2010 study published in the *Journal of Injury Prevention* examined six Montreal protected bike lanes, also known as cycle tracks, and found that these streets had reduced injury rates of 28 percent compared with similar streets without protected bicycle infrastructure. As of 2015, 150 miles (241 km) of Montreal's 400 miles (644 km) of bike lanes were physically separated from motor vehicle traffic.

Since 2006, Seville, Spain, has installed more than 81 miles (130 km) of protected bike lanes—and the results speak for themselves. The Institute for Transportation & Development Policy reports that, between 2006 and 2012, the number of daily cyclists went from 5,000 to 72,000 per day and from a rate of less than 0.5 percent of trips to around 7 percent.

Bicycle infrastructure is being erected all over the world, with examples including 87 miles (140 km) of bikeways—much of it physically segregated from motor traffic—built in Buenos Aires, Argentina, between 2012 and 2015, and plans to construct the world's longest single protected bike lane, measuring 114 miles (184 km), across five provinces in Thailand by 2017.

FIGURE 3

Federal Funds Budgeted for Bike Lanes and Other Projects

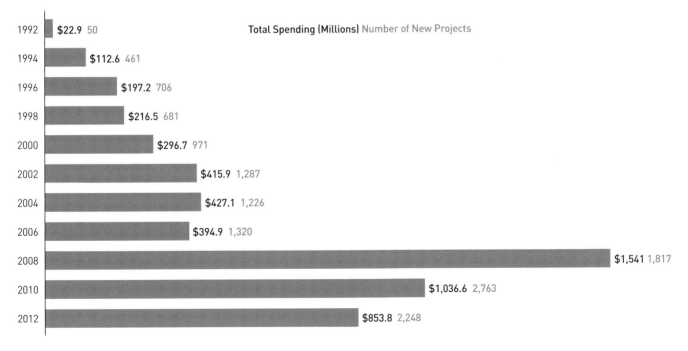

Source: Federal Highway Administration.

BICYCLE SHARING

Another infrastructure investment that has helped active transportation go mainstream is the development of bicycle-sharing systems. Bicycle sharing is a service in which bikes are made available for shared use by individuals on a short-term basis.

Bike-share systems allow people to borrow a bicycle from one place and return it to another. To encourage the use of bicycles, many bike-share systems offer memberships that make the first 30 to 45 minutes free or very inexpensive. This allows each bike to be used by several riders per day.

In 2004, there were just 13 large municipal bike-share systems worldwide. This figure increased to more than 800 as of 2015, with over 200 in China alone. Some of the largest bicycle-sharing systems are in China, where the city of Wuhan had 90,000 bikes as of 2014. The largest bike-share system outside China is in Paris, where the Vélib' system offers over 21,000 bicycles at 1,800 stations.

Bike sharing is now growing rapidly in North America, with more than 50 systems launched between 2010 and 2015. The largest bike-share system as of 2015 in the United States is New York City's CitiBike, with more than 7,500 bicycles and 460 stations. Mexico City's ECOBICI had 6,600 bikes and 444 stations as of 2015.

For more information on bicycle sharing, see the "Bicycle Sharing" profile on page 54.

Bike-share stations allow users to cycle between employment destinations and residential and commercial areas. *(Shutterstock/ Ekaterina Pokrovsky)*

Becoming Bicycle Friendly

What does it take to create a bicycle-friendly community? Obviously, providing bike infrastructure is the first step, but other factors are important as well. The League of American Bicyclists says that no single route to becoming a "bicycle-friendly community" exists. No two communities are the same, and each can capitalize on its strengths to make biking better and safer, but the league recommends five key "Essential Elements of a Bicycle-Friendly America":

>> **Engineering.** Have facilities been built to promote cycling in the community? What is the total mileage of the bicycle network, both on-road and off-road? Do arterial streets have bike lanes? What is the availability of bike parking? Signals? Repair shops? Does the bike network connect to major community destinations like schools, neighborhoods, and the downtown?

>> **Encouragement.** Does the community promote and encourage cycling through events, campaigns, and incentives? Is there a bicycle club? A bicycle advisory committee? A bicycle advocacy organization? Does the community promote a bike-to-work day, week, or month?

>> **Education.** Does the community do education about bike safety for both cyclists and motorists? Is there a community-wide bike map? How about bicycle-skills classes on repairs and ridership? Is the community aware of the location of bike trails and other facilities?

>> **Enforcement.** Does the community have bicycle-friendly laws and policies in place? Does the community use enforcement to encourage cyclists to obey the laws and motorists to share the road? Do police patrol the bike trails? Are they plowed during the winter?

>> **Evaluation and planning.** Does the community know how many people cycle and for what reasons? Is the bike plan current? Is it being implemented? Should it be updated? Is there a bike program coordinator or staff person? Does the city have data on ridership, crashes, and fatalities?

Bicycling is becoming an increasingly popular transportation option for commuters around the world. (Shutterstock/Mikael Damkier)

BICYCLE-FRIENDLY BUSINESSES

Businesses, building owners, and developers are all starting to recognize and respond to the growing interest in active transportation. The League of American Bicyclists' Bicycle-Friendly Business Program now lists more than 1,090 bicycle-friendly businesses in 49 states.

Through this program, businesses are recognized for their efforts to encourage their employees and customers to ride bikes. The list of bicycle-friendly businesses has grown from just a handful a few years ago to a long list that now includes businesses both big and small.

Today, companies like Target, Facebook, Kimberly-Clark, and the DaVita Corporation have joined hundreds of small businesses, nonprofit groups, and universities on the growing list of bicycle-friendly businesses.

Employers say that bicycling can create healthier employees who are more energetic, alert, and productive, and building owners say that bike-friendly buildings can help attract tenants, residents, and customers while also providing a value premium.

Becoming a bicycle-friendly business is relatively inexpensive and easy; it starts with the infrastructure. Some of the key features that bike-friendly businesses provide, as explained by the league, include the following:

>> **Bike parking.** Ample secure, convenient, and high-quality bicycle parking for employees and guests.

>> **Shower and locker facilities.** Showers, lockers, and changing areas provided for employees.

>> **Bike repair areas.** Tools, supplies, and a work stand for employees to use.

Bicycling infrastructure can connect people to recreational destinations such as beaches. (Shutterstock/PerseoMedusa)

>> **Shared bikes.** Shared bicycles that staff can use for noncommute trips, like running errands or going to meetings.

>> **Easy access.** Easy access by bike from a network of dedicated bikeways or low-traffic streets.

As shown in the project profiles that follow in chapters 2 and 3, residential and commercial developers are recognizing the value of trail-oriented development and we are now seeing a new generation of bicycle-friendly buildings and projects.

By adding bike-friendly amenities, developers and homebuilders are finding that they can appeal to both ends of the demographic spectrum: young people who want to live closer to work as well as baby boomers who are looking for a more walkable and bikable lifestyle.

Trail-Oriented Development

Infrastructure—the physical facilities and systems that support economic activity—is a key driver of real estate investment and development. Historically, real estate was influenced by the quality and location of roads, bridges, and other forms of auto-oriented infrastructure. The Interstate Highway System, for example, was a critical factor in the growth of suburban America.

More recently, *transit-oriented development* has become a common term in the lexicon of real estate and transportation officials. Transit-oriented development is characterized by compact, mixed-use, residential, and commercial development that is clustered around a transit stop or a rail station. Today, bike trails, bike lanes, bike-share systems, and other forms of active transportation infrastructure are helping spur a new generation of "trail-oriented development." This trend reflects the desire of people around the world to live in places where driving an automobile is just one of a number of safe, convenient, and affordable transportation options. The Urban Land Institute's *America in 2015* report found that, in the United States, over half of all people (52 percent) and 63 percent of millennials would like to live in a place where they do not need to use a car very often; half of U.S. residents believe their communities need more bike lanes.

The detailed case studies that follow illustrate the many types of residential and commercial development that are leveraging bicycle and pedestrian infrastructure to create popular and profitable projects and places.

Above: Bicycle traffic signals can improve road safety by giving cyclists extra time to cross busy intersections. *(Shutterstock/ Carsten Medom Madsen)*

Below: Cities such as Berlin are improving bicycle routes to accommodate an influx of residents and development projects. *(Shutterstock/pixelklex)*

Active Transportation and Quality of Life

Would you prefer to live in a community where you have to drive everywhere for everything? Or would you prefer to live in a community where you could walk, ride a bicycle, take public transportation, or drive to get where you want to go? The growth in the popularity of walking and bicycling is a result of many factors, but at its core it is about people choosing a lifestyle that gives them more options and requires less dependence on motor vehicles.

Since its inception, the federal and state governments in the United States have spent approximately $5 trillion to build and maintain the Interstate Highway System. Until recently, federal investments in bicycle and pedestrian infrastructure amounted to less than a tenth of 1 percent of this amount. Now, governments at all levels are rediscovering the value of active transportation, and the creation of bicycle infrastructure is prompting real estate development.

The long-range potential of cycling as a mode of transportation is immense. According to the Rails-to-Trails Conservancy, if the United States doubled the current 1 percent of all trips by bicycle to 2 percent, the country would collectively save more than 693 million gallons (2.6 billion liters) of gasoline each year. The United States would also cut air pollution, lower carbon emissions, and greatly improve public health.

According to the Institute of Transportation Studies at the University of California–Davis, in every country, at least 35 percent of trips are under 3.1 miles (5 km), which is equivalent to a 20-minute ride on a bicycle. However, less than 7 percent of urban trips globally are taken on a bike. If 23 percent of trips were taken on bikes by 2050, the world would avoid 300 megatons of CO_2 emissions, leading to a cumulative savings of $25 trillion between 2015 and 2050.

The value of cycling has already been demonstrated in bicycle-friendly communities across the globe. Cities that have invested in bike infrastructure have reaped economic and development returns. And, as this report shows, developers who have responded to this trend are being rewarded with both plaudits and profits.

CHAPTER 2

Real Estate Development Projects

Is there market demand for projects that cater to people who ride bicycles? What is the value of access to trails, bike lanes, and sidewalks for developers? How are bike-friendly features being used to position real estate developments in a competitive marketplace?

This chapter profiles development projects that have active transportation components at the core of their identities. The profiles illustrate how developers are choosing sites along popular bicycling and walking routes and including bicycle-friendly amenities in their projects. The profiles show how these amenities have helped meet overall development objectives and also include insights from developers on the rationale for investing in active transportation features.

Eight of the projects profiled in this chapter are located in the United States, with additional case studies from London and Singapore. Projects range from a large mixed-use complex in a world capital to a smaller workforce housing development in a medium-sized market. While a wide diversity of projects is included, they share themes regarding the specific active transportation features included and the value of these investments.

The projects highlighted herein are at the leading edge of efforts to take advantage of civic investment in bicycling facilities, such as trails and bike lanes, and growing market demand for bike-friendly places. They were identified through input from a variety of ULI sources.

Shared themes among profiled projects include the following:

>> **Trails, bike lanes, bike-share stations, and sidewalks add value to development projects.** Developers associated with the profiled projects explained that locations along active transportation routes were highly desirable due to increased project visibility, the growth in the popularity of car-free commuting, and the desire of potential tenants to have access to opportunities to live healthier lifestyles.

>> **Overview of Development Profiles**

Project	Location	Use	Dedicated bicycle storage areas	Extra-wide hallways or bike elevators
Bici Flats	Des Moines, IA	Multifamily	X	X
Circa	Indianapolis, IN	Multifamily	X	
Flats at Bethesda Avenue	Bethesda, MD	Mixed use	X	X
Gotham West	New York, NY	Mixed use	X	
Hassalo on Eighth	Portland, OR	Mixed use	X	
MoZaic	Minneapolis, MN	Mixed use	X	
Ponce City Market	Atlanta, GA	Mixed use	X	X
Silver Moon Lodge	Albuquerque, NM	Mixed use	X	
250 City Road	London, UK	Mixed use	X	X
Westwood Residences	Singapore	Mutifamily	X	

>> **A market for the inclusion of bike-friendly features in residential and commercial properties exists and is growing.** There is demand for accommodating bicycles in apartments, offices, and commercial spaces. Developers have found that tenants of buildings close to active transportation corridors expect to be able to own, maintain, and have easy access to bicycles on site and that this trend is expanding across age groups.

>> **Relatively small investments in bike-friendly amenities can lead to improved returns.** Many of the developments that have included bike-friendly features have experienced faster-than-expected lease-up rates, rental rate premiums over market peers, and, in some cases, the ability to market properties outside city centers as easily accessible to urban cores via trails and bike lanes.

>> **A reciprocal relationship exists between the private and public sectors in terms of maximizing investments in active transportation.** Developers have benefited from the ability to build in sought-after locations that are close to publicly financed active transportation routes, but have also made direct investments in active transportation by partially financing improvements to facilities, such as trail networks or bike-sharing systems, via public/private partnerships.

>> **Approaches to accommodating active transportation in development projects can be grouped into ten categories.** Shown in the figure below, many of the active transportation–friendly features included in the profiled developments were common across project type, market size, and location. All projects provided dedicated bicycle storage, and many accommodated on-site bicycle repairs.

The projects highlighted in this publication show that leading development practitioners are recognizing the potential of the competitive advantage to be gained by investing in active transportation amenities. By leveraging and enhancing access to walking and bicycling facilities, they are helping initiate a win-win cycle of mutually reinforcing private and public sector investment in active transportation in communities around the world.

Bicycle workroom	Bike-washing station	Bike valet	Shower and/or locker facilities	Bicycle parts or mechanic available on site	Investment in on-site bike rentals or bike share	Bike park and ride	Investment in public active transportation infrastructure
X	X						
X	X				X		
						X	X
		X		X	X		
X	X	X	X	X			
			X				X
X		X	X				X
X					X		
X	X				X		X
X	X						X

Bici Flats

Des Moines, Iowa

BICI FLATS, a 154-unit multifamily development in Des Moines, Iowa, is located at the intersection of three paved trails that connect pedestrians and bicyclists to downtown. With a planned opening in 2016, Bici Flats will capitalize on its location by catering to prospective tenants who desire active lifestyles and access to urban amenities.

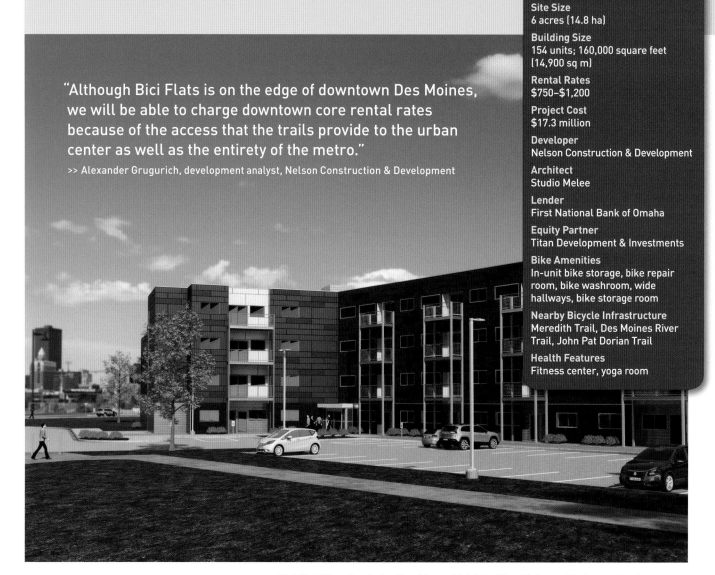

"Although Bici Flats is on the edge of downtown Des Moines, we will be able to charge downtown core rental rates because of the access that the trails provide to the urban center as well as the entirety of the metro."

>> Alexander Grugurich, development analyst, Nelson Construction & Development

Bici Flats' location in the Two Rivers District of Des Moines will give residents access to the urban core via a network of trails. *(Nelson Construction & Development)*

QUICK FACTS

Location
1405 SE First Street,
Des Moines, Iowa

Status
Under construction;
opening August 2016

Type of Project
Multifamily

Site Size
6 acres (14.8 ha)

Building Size
154 units; 160,000 square feet
(14,900 sq m)

Rental Rates
$750–$1,200

Project Cost
$17.3 million

Developer
Nelson Construction & Development

Architect
Studio Melee

Lender
First National Bank of Omaha

Equity Partner
Titan Development & Investments

Bike Amenities
In-unit bike storage, bike repair room, bike washroom, wide hallways, bike storage room

Nearby Bicycle Infrastructure
Meredith Trail, Des Moines River Trail, John Pat Dorian Trail

Health Features
Fitness center, yoga room

Context for Development

When planning for Bici Flats, developer Nelson Construction & Development looked to experiences with their existing properties and identified a market for multifamily housing just outside of the center of Des Moines. Residents at Nelson's developments noted that they were looking for locations with opportunities for walking, jogging, and bicycling.

Mike Nelson, president and owner of Nelson Construction & Development, explains that the "urban active" segment of the market is "attracted to trail access and bicycle-friendly amenities that allow them direct connections to downtown and other nearby recreational amenities."

The location of Bici Flats in the Two Rivers District, at the meeting point of the Meredith, John Pat Dorian, and Des Moines River trails, gives prospective tenants the option of a scenic walk or bicycle ride to downtown Des Moines, as well as access to open space.

All three trails provide views of the Des Moines and Raccoon rivers. The 3.1-mile (5 km) Meredith Trail connects Bici Flats to downtown Des Moines and forms a portion of 8.8 miles (14.2 km) of paved downtown loop trails. The trails also form connections to many of the 52 miles (84 km) of trails within city limits and 550 miles (885 km) in the larger region.

Alexander Grgurich, development analyst at Nelson Construction & Development, notes that "although Bici Flats is on the edge of downtown Des Moines, we will be able to charge downtown core rental rates because of the access that the trails provide to the urban center as well as the entirety of the metro."

Active Transportation–Friendly Features

In order to capitalize on the project's nearby trail infrastructure, Nelson Construction & Development worked to create a building that accommodates bike ownership. Active transportation–friendly features include the following:

>> **Bicycle storage room.** There will be keycard-protected space for 125 bikes in the basement of the building.
>> **In-unit bicycle storage.** Front closet "mud rooms" will be able to accommodate bikes both horizontally and vertically, or residents can choose to store bicycles on the patios or balconies included in every unit.
>> **Wide hallways.** At 82 inches (208 cm) wide, hallways will be ten inches (25 cm) wider than the standard size, and tenants will be able to easily transport bicycles through the building.
>> **Bike workroom.** A room that provides residents with access to work stands, basic bike repair tools, and air pumps will be included.
>> **Bike washing station.** Tenants will be able to clean their bikes before rolling them through the building.

Directly adjacent to Bici Flats, the Meredith Trail provides scenic views of the Des Moines skyline. *(Nelson Construction & Development)*

Bici Flats is located at the intersection of three trails that connect walkers and cyclists with downtown Des Moines. *(Nelson Construction & Development)*

Development Lessons

Bici Flats will be marketed primarily to recreational cyclists, but by facilitating bike ownership and access to active transportation routes that connect shops, restaurants, and employment centers, the development also reflects an expansion of the bicycle culture in Des Moines.

The city of Des Moines received a Bronze Award from the League of American Bicyclists in 2015 in recognition of the creation of new trails, bike parking, and bike-related events. The award, however, noted that the city has far to go in improving its on-road bicycle facilities. To that end, Des Moines approved $500,000 to add bike lanes, trail connections, and shared-lane pavement markings to downtown streets in 2015.

Bici Flats' bike-oriented development features and the local investments in bicycle infrastructure reflect the growing demand for active transportation in Des Moines.

Grgurich explains, "We look to learn from this development and how tenants will interact with the bicycle amenities and trails." As opportunities for bicycling in the area continue to grow, Nelson Construction & Development will take note of how residents make use of the bike amenities at Bici Flats and will consider adding similar features to future projects.

Circa
Indianapolis, Indiana

QUICK FACTS

Location
617 N. College Avenue,
Indianapolis, Indiana

Status
Opened in August 2014

Type of Project
Multifamily

Site Size
3.1 acres (1.2 ha)

Building Size
265 units; 295,000 square feet
(27,400 sq m) across six buildings

Rental Rates
$950–$2,500

Project Cost
$31 million

Developer
Milhaus

Architect
Blackline Studio

Lender
Regions Bank

Equity Partner
Undisclosed

Bike Amenities
Bike storage, workroom, bike
washing station, bike share

Nearby Bicycle Infrastructure
Adjacent to the Indianapolis
Cultural Trail

Health Features
Fitness center, swimming pool,
outdoor patio

CIRCA is a 265-unit multifamily development that opened in downtown Indianapolis in 2014. The project is adjacent to the Indianapolis Cultural Trail, a popular bike and pedestrian path that links vibrant downtown districts. The project's trailside location and the inclusion of bike-friendly amenities have contributed to the marketability of its units.

"The Indianapolis Cultural Trail adds tremendous value to Circa and has been the most transformative infrastructure investment in downtown Indianapolis in the last five to ten years." >> Jake D. Dietrich, director of development, Milhaus

Context for Development

Circa's units are spread across six buildings that are directly adjacent to the Indianapolis Cultural Trail, an eight-mile (13 km) path that connects shops, art galleries, restaurants, and residential areas.

Milhaus, Circa's developer, recognizes the Indianapolis Cultural Trail's status as a transportation corridor that is increasing the vitality of the local area. Jake D. Dietrich, Milhaus's director of development, notes, "The Indianapolis Cultural Trail adds tremendous value to Circa and has been the most transformative infrastructure investment in downtown Indianapolis in the last five to ten years."

Milhaus decided to include bicycle-friendly features in its development to attract what Dietrich calls "a growing market segment of tenants demanding active lifestyles and urban living."

Circa's design is intended to make it easy for residents to get anywhere in Indianapolis on a bicycle. Dietrich explained that Circa's bike-friendly amenities give it an advantage over market competitors and can make the difference between whether or not someone leases a unit, since many in the area view biking as either their primary mode of transportation or a leisure activity that is central to their lifestyle.

Milhaus believes that the relatively low-cost investment the firm has made to offer features that support bicycling has paid off, saying that "the upfront capital expenditures in bike amenities are quickly recouped by the leases that they have a direct impact on securing."

Active Transportation–Friendly Features

Reflecting its location next to the Indianapolis Cultural Trail, Circa includes a number of features to appeal to bicycle owners, including the following:

>> **Bicycle storage.** Included on the first floor of each of Circa's buildings, all storage rooms have dedicated entrances directly from the outside, which are secured by key fob entry. In total, there are 150 indoor, wall-mounted bike racks.
>> **Complimentary bike-share service.** Residents and visitors can check out bikes, helmets, and locks for use in the local area.
>> **Bike workroom.** Called the "Maker's Room," this area includes a work stand, bike-related tools, air pumps, and other supplies. The Maker's Room has a nine-foot-wide (2.7 m) garage door to allow residents to easily enter with bicycles.
>> **Bike washing station.** There is a dedicated area with hoses, scrub brushes, and buckets to wash dirty bikes.

Development Lessons

Indianapolis's downtown population grew by more than 37 percent between 2005 and 2015, and the rate of bicycle commuting in the city grew by over 101 percent between 2000 and 2014. Circa's location on the Indianapolis Cultural Trail and inclusion of bike-friendly amenities both reflect these changing circumstances and support citywide investments in bicycle infrastructure.

Further reflecting the growing popularity of active transportation in Indianapolis, Milhaus is currently developing four new multifamily residential properties close to the Indianapolis Cultural Trail.

Tadd Miller, chief executive officer of Milhaus, believes that the Indianapolis Cultural Trail and surrounding residential properties are mutually supportive, saying that "developments add users to the trail and the trail increases the quality of life at nearby developments."

Miller explains that each increase in the number of pedestrians or bicyclists on the Indianapolis Cultural Trail is also an increase in the visibility of Circa and other trail-oriented development projects. Likewise, increasing the number of residents along the trail increases use of the trail, as walking or bicycling becomes an engrained part of residents' daily lives.

Bicycle storage is included on the first floor of each of Circa's buildings. (© 2015 by Zach Dobson)

Facing page: Circa provides access for residents to the Indianapolis Cultural Trail, a popular path that links various downtown districts. (© 2015 by Zach Dobson)

Flats at Bethesda Avenue

Bethesda, Maryland

THE FLATS AT BETHESDA AVENUE is a mixed-use development in Bethesda, Maryland, that opened in 2015. The project's location along the 11-mile (17.7 km) Capital Crescent Trail, which runs among Washington, D.C., and Bethesda and Silver Spring, Maryland, gives residents the option to commute to work on a bike and attracts pedestrians and bicyclists to on-site retail establishments.

QUICK FACTS

Location
7170 Woodmont Avenue, Bethesda, Maryland

Status
Opened in 2015

Type of Project
Mixed-use

Site Size
1.4 acres (0.6 ha)

Building Size
162 residential units; 218,000 square feet (20,300 sq m), including 28,000 square feet (2,600 sq m) of retail

Rental Rates
Market-rate rents from $2,200 to over $6,500; 38 workforce units offered below market rate

Project Cost
$217 million

Developers
StonebridgeCarras LLC and PN Hoffman

Architect
SK+I Architects

Lender
Northwestern Mutual Life Insurance Company

Equity Partners
Northwestern Mutual Life and Buvermo Investments

Bike Amenities
Direct trail access, trail widening, on-site open space, bike drop-off, and bike storage

Nearby Bicycle Infrastructure
Adjacent to Capital Crescent Trail

Health Features
Fitness center, yoga room, and cardio machines

"Our residents love that they are one step from such a great D.C.-area rail trail." >> Jane G. Mahaffie, principal at StonebridgeCarras LLC

Residents of the Flats at Bethesda Avenue have direct access to the Capital Crescent Trail. *(Jane G. Mahaffie)*

Context for Development

The Flats at Bethesda Avenue consists of 162 market-rate and workforce residential units and 28,000 square feet (2,600 sq m) of retail space built on a former surface parking lot in downtown Bethesda. The development is adjacent to the Capital Crescent Trail—one of the busiest trails in the United States, with roughly 1 million users per year.

The Flats at Bethesda Avenue was created through a public/private partnership between Montgomery County and developers StonebridgeCarras LLC and PN Hoffman. This arrangement led to a project that leverages its trail-adjacent location to support retail tenants and accommodate active transportation.

Jane G. Mahaffie, principal at StonebridgeCarras, notes, "Immediate access of our residents and retail tenants to the Capital Crescent Trail is a fabulous amenity. Retail tenants Chop't and Paul Bakery have frontage immediately to the trail, and the outdoor seating areas of all our restaurants are quite popular as a trail stop."

Mahaffie adds, "Our residents love that they are one step from such a great D.C.-area rail trail. The Capital Crescent Trail is one facet of the premium location for the distinctive residences at the Flats at Bethesda Avenue."

The Flats at Bethesda Avenue's location along the Capital Crescent Trail serves residents who commute by bike, due to the trail's access to Washington, D.C., and connections to other regional trails, including the C&O Canal Towpath and the Rock Creek Trail. A planned light-rail line, called the Purple Line, would run between Bethesda and New Carrollton, Maryland, alongside sections of the Capital Crescent Trail and would require reconfiguring a portion of the trail in downtown Bethesda.

Active Transportation–Friendly Features

Investments in active transportation–friendly infrastructure and biking and walking amenities at the Flats at Bethesda Avenue include the following:

>> **Bicycle storage.** The Flats has a secured bike storage room for residents, which accommodates 60 bikes, with additional publicly accessible bike parking space along the trail and space for 30 bikes in the car parking garage.

>> **Direct trail access.** Residential and retail tenants can walk or ride a bike on the Capital Crescent Trail from new paths that connect directly to the property.

>> **Trail widening and improved crosswalks.** The project resulted in a widening of the Capital Crescent Trail from ten feet (3 m) to 14 feet (4.2 m) along the length of the property as well as widening of local sidewalks and narrowing of crosswalks to improve pedestrian conditions.

>> **Bicycle drop-off.** This "park and ride" system allows people using the on-site public garage to drive their cars to the Flats

The Flats at Bethesda Avenue gives retail tenants frontage directly on the Capital Crescent Trail. *(Jane G. Mahaffie)*

The Flats at Bethesda Avenue project included improvements to the Capital Crescent Trail. *(Ed McMahon)*

at Bethesda Avenue, drop off a bicycle, park their car in the underground garage, and then pick up their bicycle right outside the garage elevator so they can complete their trip on the trail. Garage elevators can also accommodate bicycles.

Development Lessons

While the Flats at Bethesda Avenue is a trail-oriented development project, it originated in Montgomery County, Maryland's desire to increase the supply of public car parking spaces in Bethesda while also encouraging mixed-use development.

The county's goals were achieved, since the project includes a new underground public parking facility that increased the supply of parking threefold, but the development also led to enhancements to the Capital Crescent Trail and nearby public space.

The combination of bike-friendly investments at the Flats at Bethesda Avenue and the increase in public car parking spaces shows how a public/private partnership can meet multiple development goals.

The widening of the Capital Crescent Trail and associated improvements to local park and active transportation space underscore the value that a trail can create in enlivening a local community and serving as a transportation corridor while also supporting residential and retail development projects.

Gotham West

New York, New York

GOTHAM WEST is a mixed-use development that opened in 2013 on the west side of midtown Manhattan. Situated near the Hudson River Greenway, Gotham West lets residents and visitors enjoy amenities that allow them to take advantage of active transportation options to reach area destinations.

QUICK FACTS

Location
550 W. 45th Street,
New York, New York

Status
Opened in August 2013

Type of Project
Mixed-use

Site Size
4 acres (1.6 ha)

Building Size
1,240 residential units; 15,000 square feet (1,400 sq m) of retail; 1.15 million total square feet (107,000 sq m)

Rental Rates
Market-rate monthly rents from $2,800 to $9,000+, affordable and middle-income units also available

Project Cost
$520 million

Developer
Gotham Organization

Architect
Schuman, Lichtenstein, Claman, & Efron

Lender
Wells Fargo

Equity Partner
Undisclosed

Bike Amenities
Bike storage, bike valet, bike shop, resident bike porter service

Nearby Bicycle Infrastructure
One block from the Hudson River Greenway

Health Features
Fitness center, spinning and yoga studio

Gotham West provides residents and visitors with bike-friendly amenities and landscaped public areas. *(Brian Park)*

Context for Development

Gotham West is a luxury mixed-use project in New York City's Hell's Kitchen neighborhood. The developer, Gotham Organization, has positioned Gotham West to cater to users of the 11-mile (18 km) Hudson River Greenway, which is just over a block away.

In addition to 1,240 residential units, Gotham West includes a retail space known as Gotham West Market that features a food hall, as well as a bike shop, with sales and on-site repairs, that provides services for residents and visitors.

Gotham West's location and bike-friendly features allowed developers to capitalize on the recent increase in bike commuting in New York City, which more than doubled between 2009 and 2013.

Christopher Jaskiewicz, chief operating officer for Gotham Organization, notes the value of the project's location, stating, "Gotham West is geared toward a healthy lifestyle, and we consider easy access to the Hudson River Greenway and its connections to additional trails and bike lanes to be a great differentiating amenity for our 3,000 residents."

Active Transportation–Friendly Features

Gotham Organization leveraged Gotham West's location near the Hudson River Greenway by including features that support bike riding for residents and visitors alike. Features include the following:

>> **On-site bike shop.** Gotham courted established New York City bike shop NYC Velo to open a branch store as part of the development, giving residents a place to have bikes repaired on site. NYC Velo also sells a range of bicycles, parts, and gear.

>> **Resident bike porter storage service.** This free service employs NYC Velo staff to store residents' bicycles on site. The storage space can accommodate up to 610 bikes.

>> **Bike rentals.** The NYC Velo bike shop offers daily bike rentals for residents and visitors.

>> **Bike parking for guests.** NYC Velo offers same-day bike storage for visitors to Gotham West Market, encouraging bike riding to the retail portion of the development.

Development Lessons

Gotham West's location was not traditionally known as a retail destination, but the inclusion of the NYC Velo bike shop at Gotham West Market was central to project objectives. In exchange for offering NYC Velo's cycling expertise and complimentary bike concierge services to residents and Gotham West Market patrons as an encouragement to visit, Gotham Organization was able to offer NYC Velo a reduced monthly rental rate.

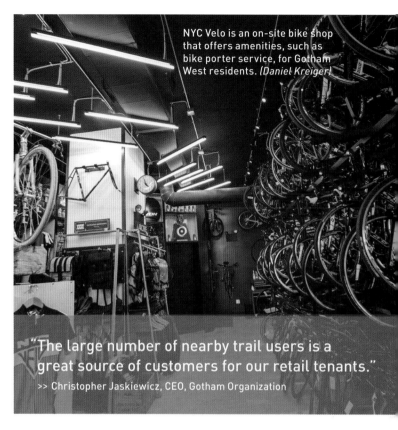

NYC Velo is an on-site bike shop that offers amenities, such as bike porter service, for Gotham West residents. *(Daniel Kreiger)*

"The large number of nearby trail users is a great source of customers for our retail tenants."
>> Christopher Jaskiewicz, CEO, Gotham Organization

The arrangement with NYC Velo, which includes same-day bike storage for visitors to the bike shop and food hall, serves to attract foot traffic to Gotham West Market from the Hudson River Greenway.

Jaskiewicz explains Gotham Organization's motivation for including the NYC Velo store and Gotham West Market as part of the development, noting, "Our location near the Greenway makes Gotham West Market the perfect pit stop for bikers, who love the bike concierge and specialists at NYC Velo."

He adds, "The large number of nearby trail users is a great source of customers for our retail tenants."

Gotham West's bicycle-oriented amenities and access to the Hudson River Greenway have contributed to the establishment of mixed-use development that supports the continuing growth in bicycle use in New York City. The Gotham West Market food hall attracts visitors to the development who can easily access its unique eateries by bicycle.

The presence of NYC Velo and its bike-oriented services for residents and market patrons illustrates how developers can work with a local business to create an innovative arrangement that supports development objectives in a context-sensitive way.

Hassalo on Eighth
Portland, Oregon

HASSALO ON EIGHTH is a mixed-use project located in Portland that includes the largest bicycle parking facility anywhere in North America. Taking advantage of its location along streets with protected bike lanes, project developers have included features that promote active transportation and sustainability, and enhance the appeal of the project.

QUICK FACTS

Location
1088 NE Seventh Avenue, Portland, Oregon

Status
Final phase opened in October 2015

Type of Project
Mixed-use

Site Size
3 acres (1.2 ha)

Building Size
657 residential units; 592,600 gross square feet (55,100 sq m) of housing, 58,100 gross square feet (5,400 sq m) of retail, and 271,600 gross square feet (25,200 sq m) of office space

Rental Rates
Average residential rate of $2.33 per square foot ($25 per sq m); apartments from $1,010 to $3,500+ per month

Project Cost
$192 million

Developer
American Assets Trust

Architect
GBD Architects

Lender
N/A

Equity Partner
N/A

Bike Amenities
Bike parking with valet, bike washing station, bike workroom, on-site repair/parts available, shower and locker room

Nearby Bicycle Infrastructure
Adjacent to protected bike lanes

Health Features
Fitness center, yoga room, boot camp classes

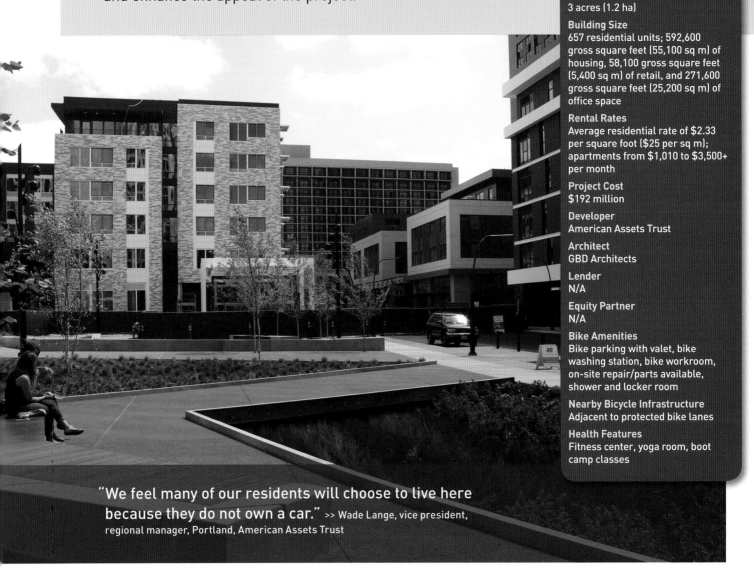

"We feel many of our residents will choose to live here because they do not own a car." >> Wade Lange, vice president, regional manager, Portland, American Assets Trust

A courtyard at Hassalo on Eighth provides residents and commuters with a place to relax. *(GBD Architects Incorporated)*

Hassalo on Eighth was built along a corner of NE Seventh Avenue and NE Multnomah Street, adjacent to protected bike lanes. *(GBD Architects Incorporated)*

Hassalo on Eighth is located in Portland's Lloyd District, just east of downtown. *(GBD Architects Incorporated)*

Context for Development

Hassalo on Eighth has helped transform the landscape of Portland, Oregon's Lloyd District, an area east of downtown, which traditionally contained mostly commercial uses. A mixed-use project built on a former surface parking lot, Hassalo consists of three buildings and 657 apartment units, making it the largest residential development in Portland to date.

As part of the "Lloyd EcoDistrict," a coalition of local organizations working to create "the most sustainable living-and-working district in North America," project developer American Assets Trust created Hassalo on Eighth with the goal of attracting residents who find the proximity to Portland's 319 miles (513 km) of bikeways attractive.

Wade Lange, vice president, regional manager, Portland, for American Assets Trust, explains, "We feel many of our residents will choose to live here because they do not want to own a car and there is no location in the city that provides better proximity to transportation options than Hassalo."

Local residents and workers have access to bike lanes and trails, as well as rail and bus transit services that accommodate bicycles. This active transportation infrastructure allows for convenient access to downtown Portland, just across the Willamette River from Hassalo.

Active Transportation–Friendly Features

American Assets Trust included innovative active transportation–friendly amenities at Hassalo on Eighth to appeal to Portland residents who ride bicycles. Features currently included or being added consist of the following:

>> **North America's largest bike parking facility.** Hassalo on Eighth has space for 1,200 bicycles, nearly 20 percent more than the 1.5 spaces per unit required by Portland law. Bike parking is spread between a "bike hub" with 820 spaces and secure storage space in the three residential buildings.

>> **On-site bike valet service.** Once operational, the bike hub facility will give tenants and local workers access to free bicycle valet service, which will also include optional bike tune-ups.

>> **Bike workroom.** Dedicated space allows residents to repair bicycles in a shared facility.

>> **Bike washing area.** Residents can wash bicycles on site in an area with a movable hose.

>> **Vending machines for replacement bike parts.** Residents can purchase parts for simple repairs from on-site machines.

>> **Shower and locker room facilities.** Local bicyclists will be able to change and shower after commuting.

Development Lessons

The U.S. Census shows that Portland's bicycle commuting rate in 2014 was 7.2 percent, more than 2.5 times the 2004 rate and the highest in the nation for major U.S. cities.

Hassalo on Eighth is positioned to support Portland's growing bicycle culture due to its location along on-street bike routes and its inclusion of bike-friendly features. Many of these amenities, including the bicycle valet service, are open not just to residents, but also to area employees.

Three months after the final phase of Hassalo on Eighth opened, American Assets Trust's Wade Lange notes that the project is seeing financial success, since the residential lease-up process was ahead of schedule.

Moving forward, project developers will take note of any additional financial benefits of Hassalo's bicycle-friendly features and will incorporate these data into future development decisions, including plans to redevelop 16 blocks in the Lloyd District.

As more local residents take up bicycling as a transportation mode, developers such as American Assets Trust are highlighting the opportunity that biking presents by incorporating bike-friendly features into their properties and aggressively promoting them to the public. Such actions show how the real estate community in Portland can both support and derive value from the growing popularity of active transportation.

MoZaic

Minneapolis, Minnesota

MOZAIC is a mixed-use office building in Minneapolis adjacent to the bustling Midtown Greenway. To leverage access to the Greenway, MoZaic's developer worked to include a pedestrian and bicyclist bridge and ramp from the project site to the path, giving walkers and cyclists direct access to the building.

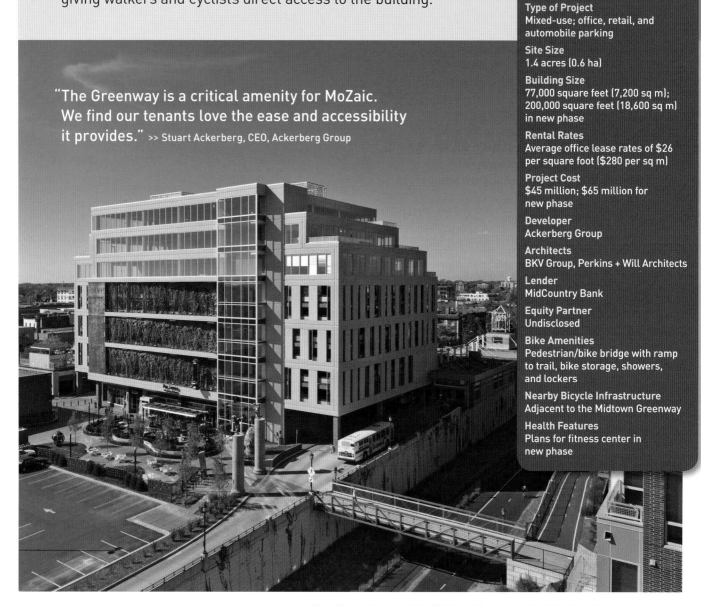

"The Greenway is a critical amenity for MoZaic. We find our tenants love the ease and accessibility it provides." >> Stuart Ackerberg, CEO, Ackerberg Group

QUICK FACTS

Location
1350 Lagoon Avenue, Minneapolis, Minnesota

Status
Opened in 2012; new phase expected to open in 2017

Type of Project
Mixed-use; office, retail, and automobile parking

Site Size
1.4 acres (0.6 ha)

Building Size
77,000 square feet (7,200 sq m); 200,000 square feet (18,600 sq m) in new phase

Rental Rates
Average office lease rates of $26 per square foot ($280 per sq m)

Project Cost
$45 million; $65 million for new phase

Developer
Ackerberg Group

Architects
BKV Group, Perkins + Will Architects

Lender
MidCountry Bank

Equity Partner
Undisclosed

Bike Amenities
Pedestrian/bike bridge with ramp to trail, bike storage, showers, and lockers

Nearby Bicycle Infrastructure
Adjacent to the Midtown Greenway

Health Features
Plans for fitness center in new phase

Located directly on Minneapolis's Midtown Greenway, MoZaic offers tenants and visitors an array of transportation options. *(Saari Photography)*

Context for Development

MoZaic is a 77,000-square-foot (7,200 sq m) office, retail, and structured automobile parking development that opened in 2012 in the Uptown area of Minneapolis. A new 200,000-square-foot (18,600 sq m) mixed-use building, called MoZaic East, is in development and is expected to open in 2017 next to the existing building.

Developed by Ackerberg Group, MoZaic provides direct access to the Midtown Greenway, a 5.5-mile (8.8 km) commuter trail in Minneapolis that sees up to 5,460 users per day.

The Midtown Greenway forms connections to the Uptown Transit Center, a bus transportation facility, as well as to other regional trails that link the neighborhood to downtown Minneapolis and surrounding areas.

The connection to the Midtown Greenway has contributed to the success of MoZaic, as Ackerberg Group's chief executive officer, Stuart Ackerberg, explains. "Whether it's walking, biking, blading, running, or boarding, the Greenway is used all the time. The Greenway is a critical amenity for MoZaic. We find our tenants love the ease and accessibility it provides."

Active Transportation–Friendly Features

MoZaic is an example of trail-oriented development, since it faces the Midtown Greenway and provides a dedicated connection to the trail. MoZaic's active transportation–friendly features in the existing and future phases of development include the following:

>> **Pedestrian and bicyclist bridge and ramp.** This bridge links MoZaic's tenants and visitors directly to the Midtown Greenway.
>> **Bicycle storage.** Plans for MoZaic East include 50 to 60 bike parking stalls for employees.
>> **Locker room with showers.** Employees who work at MoZaic East's office spaces will be able to use showers and changing rooms after riding to work.

Development Lessons

When MoZaic opened in 2012, the Uptown neighborhood lacked a significant supply of Class A office space, but Ackerberg Group believed that the area's growing stock of housing for young professionals and role as a transportation hub would support office development.

To provide direct access to MoZaic for the area's many active transportation enthusiasts, Ackerberg Group worked with local government officials and representatives from a nearby development to advance the construction of a bicycle and pedestrian ramp and bridge between MoZaic and the Midtown Greenway.

The bridge and ramp cost $370,000 and was constructed with $265,000 in funding from the Hennepin County Transit-Oriented Development program, which supports projects that encourage

Patrons of restaurants located on MoZaic's ground floor have convenient active transportation access to the building. *(Saari Photography)*

walking and bicycling. The remaining $105,000 in funding was provided by Ackerberg Group and Greco, the developer of an adjacent property.

The improved connection to MoZaic aided in its marketability. Stuart Ackerberg notes, "The ease of access to our project—including from the Midtown Greenway—definitely allowed us to charge premium rental rates. Whether employees get to the building by car, bus, [or] bike or on foot, MoZaic offers tremendously diverse transit options."

After opening, MoZaic saw immediate success and maintained a 100 percent occupancy rate as of 2016. Tenants include residential and commercial real estate companies, marketing and advertising agencies, and financial services firms.

The public/private cost-sharing agreement that resulted in the creation of the Midtown Greenway bicycle and pedestrian ramp and bridge shows how public sector transportation priorities and private development objectives can be aligned.

By investing in access to the Midtown Greenway, Ackerberg Group was able to provide a public amenity for Uptown residents and businesses that supported regional active transportation goals, while at the same time creating a facility that added value for MoZaic tenants and increased the project's overall marketability.

Ponce City Market

Atlanta, Georgia

PONCE CITY MARKET is a 2.1 million-square-foot (195,000 sq m) mixed-use redevelopment project that opened in phases between 2013 and 2015 in Atlanta. The project was built in a historic warehouse adjacent to the Atlanta BeltLine trail and incorporates numerous features to promote active transportation access.

QUICK FACTS

Location
675 Ponce de Leon Avenue NE, Atlanta, Georgia

Status
Opened in phases from 2013 to 2015

Type of Project
Mixed-use

Site Size
1.4 acres (0.6 ha)

Building Size
2.1 million square feet (195,000 sq m), 259 apartments, 330,000 square feet (30,700 sq m) of retail, 550,000 square feet (51,100 sq m) office space

Rental Rates
$1,595 to $3,500+ per month for apartments; affordable housing units also available

Project Cost
$250 million

Developer
Jamestown Companies

Architect
Nimmons, Carr, and Wright, Architects

Lenders
PNC Bank, SunTrust Bank, JP Morgan

Equity Partner
Undisclosed

Bike Amenities
Bike valet, bike storage, extra-wide hallways and elevators, on-site trail access, showers

Nearby Bicycle Infrastructure
Adjacent to the Eastside Trail, a section of the 22-mile (35 km) Atlanta Beltline

Health Features
Gym, fitness classes

"The Atlanta BeltLine is a driving force in the urbanization of Atlanta, transforming our city into a walkable, connected network of neighborhoods." >> Matt Bronfman, CEO, Jamestown

Context for Development

Along the award-winning Atlanta BeltLine, a burgeoning 22-mile (35 km) network of public parks, multiuse trails, and transit facilities, new developments geared toward car-free lifestyles are springing up. Ponce City Market is one example of this trend and is the largest redevelopment project in Atlanta since the 2008 recession.

The $250 million adaptive use project is a live/work/play development along the BeltLine's Eastside Trail. Ponce City Market transformed a former Sears building—the largest brick building in the U.S. Southeast—into a vibrant hub of activity in Atlanta's Fourth Ward neighborhood.

The mixed-use project includes 259 apartments, 550,000 square feet (51,100 sq m) of office space, a "Central Food Hall," local and national retailers, and a neighborhood school.

Jamestown Companies, the project's developer, seized the opportunity to incorporate bike-friendly features into the Ponce City Market project. Jamestown chief executive officer Matt Bronfman notes, "The Atlanta BeltLine is a driving force in the urbanization of Atlanta, transforming our city into a walkable, connected network of neighborhoods. Ponce City Market's direct connection to the BeltLine is one of the best amenities we have to offer our community. It is not only an easy way to access the market's amenities, it also provides our tenants with a great green space that connects them directly with growing neighborhoods like Virginia Highland."

Bronfman adds, "We look forward to the continued development of the BeltLine and are committed to supporting the BeltLine's efforts."

Active Transportation–Friendly Features

Active transportation–friendly features form a central component of the Ponce City Market project, and include the following:

>> **Bicycle storage.** Five hundred bicycle parking spaces are provided for residents and visitors in a secure facility.

>> **Bicycle valet service.** Visitors to the development can ride up to the building and leave their bikes with the entrance valet free of charge.

>> **Bike workroom.** Residents have access to a space where they can repair bicycles in a shared facility.

>> **Extra-wide hallways to accommodate bikes.** Residents and visitors can maneuver bicycles around the property because of the width of hallways.

>> **Elevators that can accommodate bikes.** Elevators are large enough to accommodate bicycles in standard positions.

>> **Showers for bicycle commuters.** Office workers and residents have access to a shower facility to use after commuting by bike.

Facing page: Ponce City Market offers direct BeltLine access from the building. *(Sarah Dorio)*

Ponce City Market includes a number of features to accommodate bicycling for residents, office tenants, and shoppers. *(Sarah Dorio)*

>> **Direct BeltLine access from the building and public plaza.** A walkway connection among the trail, the new public plaza, and the development provides active transportation access to pedestrians and bicyclists.

>> **Funding for the BeltLine from car parking fees.** Jamestown worked with parking provider Parkmobile to create a payment system where the first $1 of each car parking session is donated to the Atlanta BeltLine project.

Development Lessons

As of 2015, over $400 million had been invested into the Atlanta BeltLine project from public and private sources, leading to more than $2.4 billion in private development along the BeltLine corridor. Jamestown's $250 million investment in Ponce City Market is a prime example of the BeltLine's capacity to spur development.

By 2016, over 90 percent of the office space at Ponce City Market had been leased, and the retail portion of the project had attracted a mix of restaurants and shops, most of which were new to the area. The Central Food Hall features an international array of eateries run by prominent chefs and local food purveyors. The apartment units, known as the "Flats at Ponce City Market," include modern designs and features from the original structure.

Ponce City Market's combination of bike-friendly residential, office, and retail space has aided in the continuing revitalization of the surrounding neighborhood. As a result, Jamestown is investing in redeveloping an additional local property adjacent to the BeltLine, which will feature a 60,000-square-foot (5,600 sq m) grocery store and 360,000 square feet (33,400 sq m) of office space with direct trail access.

The investments that Jamestown has made in the area show the catalytic potential of active transportation infrastructure and demonstrate how developers can leverage investments in trail projects to aid in the creation of modern, high-end mixed-use projects.

Silver Moon Lodge

Albuquerque, New Mexico

SILVER MOON LODGE is a mixed-use workforce housing development located at the periphery of Albuquerque's central business district, along historic Route 66. It was designed to take advantage of nearby urban amenities as well as proximity to the city's growing bikeway network.

"There is a strong market in downtown Albuquerque for apartments that cater to pedestrians and bicyclists."

>> Jessie Lucero, property manager, Silver Moon Lodge

Located in central Albuquerque, Silver Moon Lodge offers convenient access to downtown amenities. (Dekker/Perich/Sabatini)

Silver Moon Lodge features a central bike storage facility on the ground floor of the building. *(Dekker/Perich/Sabatini)*

Residents at Silver Moon Lodge who do not own cars are able to get around on foot or by bicycle. *(Dekker/Perich/Sabatini)*

Context for Development

Silver Moon Lodge, a mixed-use development with 154 studio and one-bedroom units of workforce housing, was built for renters seeking a car-optional lifestyle in central Albuquerque.

The project is located adjacent to new bike lanes and designated cycling routes that provide easy access to the city's 400 miles (644 km) of trails, including the 16-mile (26 km) Paseo del Bosque Trail, which connects downtown Albuquerque to area destinations, including the Rio Grande Conservation Center.

Jessie Lucero, Silver Moon Lodge's property manager, explains how the project's location adds to its value, saying, "Everything our tenants need is within walking or bicycling distance. Our downtown location near trails and along the Central Avenue bike lanes allows residents to get to work, the grocery store, or to go out to eat on foot or by bicycle."

Silver Moon Lodge was built using New Mexico Mortgage Finance Authority tax credits. The annual incomes of eligible renters are capped at $26,460 per year for one person or $30,240 for units housing two people.

Residents of Silver Moon Lodge who cannot afford to own a car, or who choose not to do so, are able to get around on foot or by bicycle. The project is also located near a bus stop and on-site car-share station, further enhancing the convenience of the development for car-free households.

Active Transportation–Friendly Features

Silver Moon Lodge has several bike-friendly features for residents and visitors, including the following:

>> **A bike storage room.** The development can accommodate 50 bikes in a central facility on the ground floor of the building.
>> **Bike repair room.** Residents have access to a dedicated space with tools, air pumps, and a work stand that allows them to make repairs to bikes without having to leave the property.

>> **Resident bike-share program.** Silver Moon Lodge provides bicycles that residents can borrow on a short-term basis to run local errands.

Development Lessons

Silver Moon Lodge's bike accommodations and the nearby bicycle infrastructure support the growing local popularity of active transportation, evidenced by Albuquerque's 92 percent increase in bicycle commuting between 2012 and 2014, according to the U.S. Census.

Further supporting the use of bicycles as everyday transportation is the fact that Silver Moon Lodge's developer, GSL Properties, included just 23 car parking spots on site.

By law, GSL Properties could have proposed more than 150 spaces for cars. However, by providing fewer, the developer was able to reduce the site costs associated with building parking and instead focused on providing features that would appeal to those who want the option not to own a car.

Lucero explains that the relatively low rate of parking provision coupled with the project's bike-friendly features has aided in development objectives, saying, "There is only one car parking space for every six units, but parking has not been an issue because so many of our residents have chosen to rely on bikes to get around."

Lucero adds, "Over 95 percent of our units are occupied. There is a strong market in downtown Albuquerque for apartments that cater to pedestrians and bicyclists."

Silver Moon Lodge meets a need for high-quality affordable housing in downtown Albuquerque, as demonstrated by the fact that the building is consistently nearly fully leased.

The development's bike-friendly design caters to those who do not wish to use an automobile as their primary means of transportation and supports the shift toward bicycle commuting in the local area.

250 City Road
London, United Kingdom

250 CITY ROAD is a high-end mixed-use project in London located along designated cycling routes. The project will provide accommodations intended for the area's growing bicycle ownership and use.

"The demand for secure cycle parking will only increase in the coming years, so 'overprovision' seems sensible and will futureproof the development."
>> Christopher Abel, development director, Berkeley Group

Context for Development

A large mixed-use project with 930 high-end, luxury residential units and other uses, 250 City Road is under construction in the London Borough of Islington.

Berkeley Group, the project developer, worked with local government officials and architecture firm Foster + Partners to create a suite of bicycle-oriented amenities that will support two-wheeled commutes. Agreements between Berkeley and the Borough of Islington have led to increased investments in the area's cycling infrastructure.

Christopher Abel, Berkeley's development director, explains the motivations behind accommodating bicycle transportation, saying, "We see the additional measures . . . as not only assisting cyclists who will live and work [at 250 City Road], but as raising the standard for future development across London."

The 250 City Road project is being constructed adjacent to an existing public "Santander Cycles" bike-share station and is located near designated on-road cycle routes. These routes will help connect the project to the 18-mile (29 km) "East–West Cycle Superhighway" being built as part of a £160 million (US$240 million) system of London segregated bike lanes.

Active Transportation–Friendly Features

A number of features will be included at 250 City Road that facilitate walking, bike ownership, and commuting, including the following:

>> **Bike storage.** There will be 1,486 bike parking spaces located in a secure basement facility accessible by residents and office workers. Additional bike parking will be provided in an on-site park for use by the public.

>> **Bicycle elevators.** Three dedicated bicycle elevators will connect the underground bicycle storage space with the street level.

>> **Bike workrooms.** Space will be provided for residents to clean and maintain bikes on site.

>> **Public bike-share station.** There is an adjacent existing public bike-share station, but project developers are contributing £185,000 (US$264,559) to Transport for London, the local governmental body responsible for transportation throughout the region, for an additional 24-bike Santander Cycles station on site.

>> **Investments in on-road safety.** Berkeley is making a £20,000 (US$28,721) financial contribution to Transport for London for off-site pedestrian and bicyclist-focused safety improvements to nearby intersections.

Facing page: The 250 City Road project will feature on-site bike-share stations and promote active transportation access. *(Berkeley Homes, North East London)*

Residents and visitors to 250 City Road will be able to relax in central courtyards. *(Berkeley Homes, North East London)*

Development Lessons

The 250 City Road project's bike-friendly features and the improvements to London's cycling routes support the high rate of bike commuting in the area. The 2011 U.K. Census found that more people ride a bike to work in the London Borough of Islington—where 250 City Road is located—than drive (5.9 percent of locals cycle to work versus 5.5 percent who rely on automobiles).

To accommodate local cyclists, 250 City Road will have dedicated storage space for 1,486 bicycles—a ratio of almost 1.6 spaces per residential unit. In contrast, the project has only 200 car parking spaces.

The number of bike parking spaces exceeds the 1,223 required by London's bike-friendly zoning laws, while the number of car parking spaces is significantly less than the maximum number of spaces allowed—roughly one per unit.

Abel explains that Berkeley decided to provide ample bike parking because ". . . the demand for secure cycle parking will only increase in the coming years, so 'overprovision' seems sensible and will futureproof the development."

The project's focus on improving the safety and convenience of bicycling, and the partnership with local government to invest in improvements, show how development objectives can go hand-in-hand with municipal efforts to enhance active transportation options.

The project is emblematic of the shift toward bicycling as an everyday mode of transportation and demonstrates that bike-friendly design features can be a component of a package of luxury amenities for mixed-use developments.

Westwood Residences

Singapore

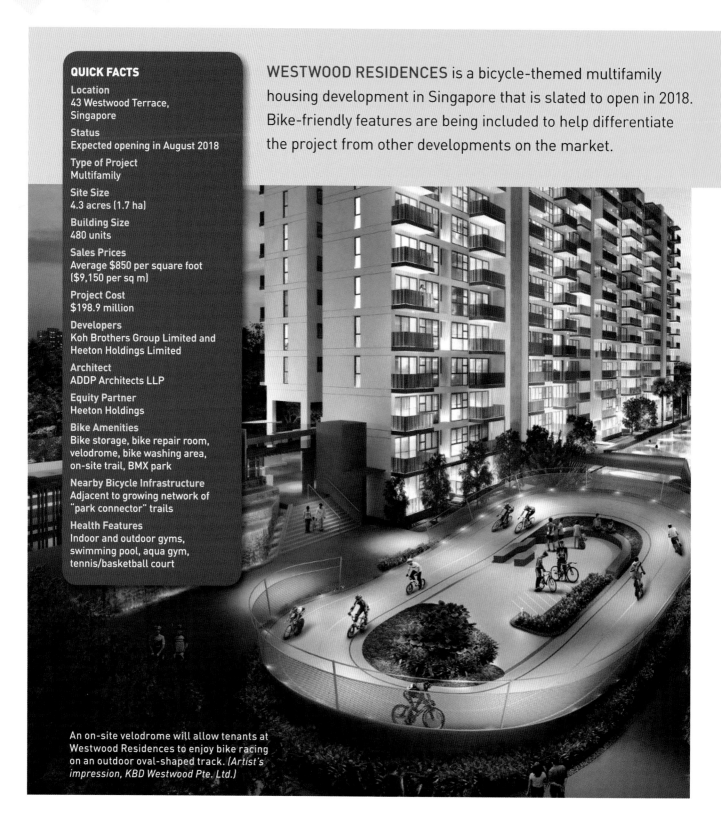

WESTWOOD RESIDENCES is a bicycle-themed multifamily housing development in Singapore that is slated to open in 2018. Bike-friendly features are being included to help differentiate the project from other developments on the market.

QUICK FACTS

Location
43 Westwood Terrace, Singapore

Status
Expected opening in August 2018

Type of Project
Multifamily

Site Size
4.3 acres (1.7 ha)

Building Size
480 units

Sales Prices
Average $850 per square foot ($9,150 per sq m)

Project Cost
$198.9 million

Developers
Koh Brothers Group Limited and Heeton Holdings Limited

Architect
ADDP Architects LLP

Equity Partner
Heeton Holdings

Bike Amenities
Bike storage, bike repair room, velodrome, bike washing area, on-site trail, BMX park

Nearby Bicycle Infrastructure
Adjacent to growing network of "park connector" trails

Health Features
Indoor and outdoor gyms, swimming pool, aqua gym, tennis/basketball court

An on-site velodrome will allow tenants at Westwood Residences to enjoy bike racing on an outdoor oval-shaped track. *(Artist's impression, KBD Westwood Pte. Ltd.)*

Context for Development

Westwood Residences is a 480-unit executive condominium (EC) project in the Jurong West area of Singapore. ECs are a type of housing in Singapore that are built and sold by private developers, but feature price points lower than market rates due to government subsidies. These hybrid public/private housing units have strict income levels for buyers and cannot be sold or rented for five years after owners take possession.

As of 2015, Singapore was experiencing a slowdown in its EC market. In order to set Westwood Residences apart from other projects and leverage new bicycle infrastructure being built by the city, the project's developers, Koh Brothers Group Limited and Heeton Holdings Limited, decided to focus on providing bike-friendly amenities for prospective residents. Westwood Residences is spending upwards of SGD$1.5 million (US$1,050,000) on the project's active transportation–themed offerings.

Danny Low, Heeton Holdings' chief operating officer and executive director, explains the rationale behind Westwood Residences' bike theme, stating, "In today's challenging operating environment, it is vital to inject unique attributes to differentiate our developments to increasingly discerning and demanding buyers in the EC market."

Low adds, "The introduction of a bike-themed development is well timed as the government intends to build more parks in the vicinity. On top of this, we will also be well poised to capitalize on the trend of more people seeking an active and healthy lifestyle."

Active Transportation–Friendly Features

Westwood Residences will include a number of features to accommodate bicycling for recreation and transportation purposes, including the following:

>> **Bicycle storage.** A facility with space to park 500 bikes will be included in the development and will feature closed-circuit television and biometric scanning to ensure that bicycles are secure.

>> **Bike workroom.** A maintenance facility for residents will include tools, tire pumps, air compressors, bike racks, and repair stands.

>> **Bike washing area.** The bicycle maintenance room will feature a dedicated area for residents to clean bikes.

>> **Bicycle velodrome.** Residents will have access to an outdoor oval-shaped bike racing track.

>> **On-site bicycle trail.** A bicycle trail will connect cyclists to parks and the burgeoning local network of trails.

>> **BMX bike park.** The development will feature a track for youth to practice BMX skills and stunts.

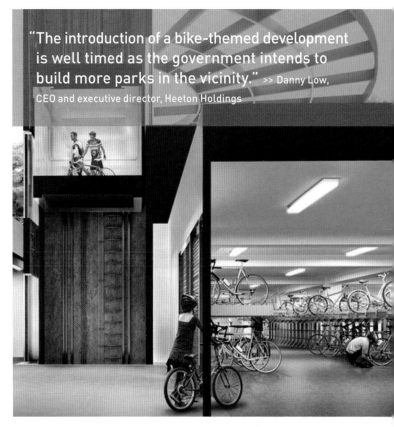

"The introduction of a bike-themed development is well timed as the government intends to build more parks in the vicinity." >> Danny Low, CEO and executive director, Heeton Holdings

Secure storage for 500 bicycles will be provided at Westwood Residences. *(Artist's impression, KBD Westwood Pte. Ltd.)*

Development Lessons

Singapore is building bicycle infrastructure to reduce automobile traffic and increase active transportation opportunities for local residents. In 2011, only 1 percent of all trips in Singapore were by bicycle, but the government aims to increase this figure by creating safer and more convenient bike routes.

As of 2015, Singapore had 143 miles (230 km) of bike paths, but the government is planning to increase that figure to 434 miles (700 km) by 2030.

"Park connector" trails near Westwood Residences link commercial and residential areas, and also form connections with multiple rail transit stations. The bike trails at Westwood Residences will provide access to the Jurong Lake District, the largest planned commercial and recreational hub outside of Singapore's central business district.

Due to its bike-friendly design and location near a growing network of trails, Westwood Residences is a unique product for the Singapore EC market. Presales of units at Westwood Residences began in May 2015, with 120 units sold on the first day. According to Channel News Asia, this is a faster rate of sale than that seen in other such developments around the same time.

The success of the project relative to that of other ECs will provide lessons on the market viability of including bike-friendly amenities in local development projects, as Singapore's active transportation infrastructure network continues to expand.

CHAPTER 3

Catalytic Bicycle and Pedestrian Infrastructure Projects

In what way do trails, bike lanes, and bicycle-sharing systems shape regional economies? What is the relationship between the real estate market and investments in active transportation infrastructure? How can public sector health and environmental goals be aligned with emerging private sector development objectives?

This chapter examines catalytic active transportation infrastructure projects, such as trails, bike lane networks, and bike-sharing systems that support and, in some instances, spur real estate development opportunities. The profiles outline investments made by the public sector, or by partnerships between the public and private sectors, that support improvements to the safety and convenience of walking and bicycling.

The projects included show how active transportation infrastructure can have positive economic impacts for cities and regions, while supporting public health and environmental goals and creating opportunities for the real estate industry to develop bicyclist- and pedestrian-friendly projects.

Key Economic and Quality-of-Life Benefits of Active Transportation Infrastructure

Property Values	Public Health and Environment	Economic Development
Properties within ¼ mile (0.4 km) of the Radnor Trail, part of Philadelphia's Circuit regional trail network, were valued on average $69,000 higher than other area properties.	Barcelona's bike-share system contributes to reducing yearly CO_2 emissions by an estimated 9,000 metric tons (9,221 tons) and leads to the equivalent of 12 lives saved each year due to increased physical activity.	Copenhagen, Denmark, predicts that completing a network of 28 "cycle superhighways" will lead to an economic return of 19 percent for the region.
Homes in Montreal saw an average increase of CA$8,649.80 (US$6,123.10) in their values after the installation of local bike-share stations.	Positive public health and environmental outcomes from London's "cycle superhighway" project will lead to a net £76 million (US$109 million) economic benefit over the next 30 years.	Minneapolis's Midtown Greenway has catalyzed more than $750 million worth of new residential development.

[Copenhagen Cycle Superhighways]

Four of the five infrastructure projects profiled in this chapter expanded and improved trail systems or bike lane networks, while the fifth highlights recent investments in public bike-sharing programs. The case studies explore initiatives in the United States, Canada, Europe, and Asia, and range from municipal projects that were initiated due to pressure from local community groups, to multidecade wholesale transformations of regional transportation systems that include dozens of public and private sector partners.

The projects included in this chapter are indicative of a worldwide trend of civic and private sector investment in active transportation facilities, and the growing market demand for walkable and bikable places. They were identified through input from a variety of ULI sources.

Shared themes among profiled projects include the following:

>> **Active transportation infrastructure can catalyze real estate development.** Trails, bike lanes, and bicycle-sharing systems can improve pedestrian and bicyclist access to employment centers, recreational destinations, and public transit facilities, thereby enhancing the attractiveness of developments along active transportation corridors. In some cases, former industrial districts and towns outside urban cores have benefited from active transportation infrastructure due to improved walking and cycling connectivity.

>> **Investments in trails, bike lanes, and bicycle-sharing systems have high levels of return on investment.** Regions and cities have found that relatively small investments in active transportation can have outsized economic returns due to improved health and environmental outcomes and reduced negative externalities, such as automobile traffic congestion and poor air quality.

>> **There is evidence of a correlation between access to active transportation facilities and increased property values.** In a number of markets, both urban and suburban, studies have found that direct access to trails, bike-sharing systems, and bike lanes can have a positive impact on property values. A number of current and recent development projects have cited this phenomenon as a rationale for investing in particular locations and/or including bike-friendly features.

>> **A reciprocal relationship exists between the private and public sectors in terms of maximizing investments in active transportation.** Developers have benefited from the ability to build in sought-after locations that are close to publicly financed active transportation routes, but have also made direct investments in active transportation by partially financing improvements to facilities, such as trail networks or bike-sharing systems, through public/private partnerships.

The Circuit Trails

Southeastern Pennsylvania and southern New Jersey

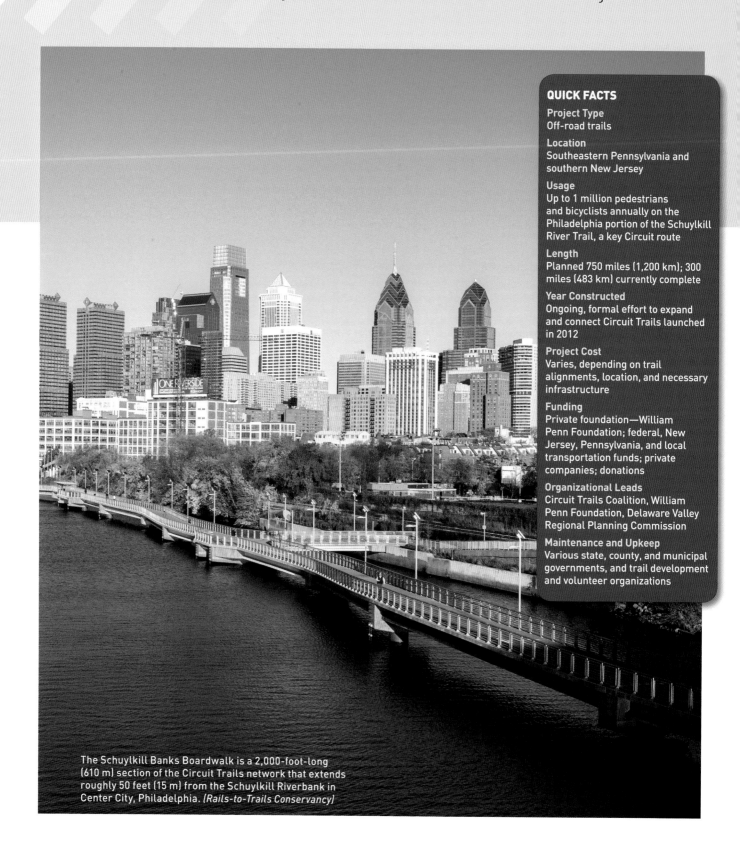

QUICK FACTS

Project Type
Off-road trails

Location
Southeastern Pennsylvania and southern New Jersey

Usage
Up to 1 million pedestrians and bicyclists annually on the Philadelphia portion of the Schuylkill River Trail, a key Circuit route

Length
Planned 750 miles (1,200 km); 300 miles (483 km) currently complete

Year Constructed
Ongoing, formal effort to expand and connect Circuit Trails launched in 2012

Project Cost
Varies, depending on trail alignments, location, and necessary infrastructure

Funding
Private foundation—William Penn Foundation; federal, New Jersey, Pennsylvania, and local transportation funds; private companies; donations

Organizational Leads
Circuit Trails Coalition, William Penn Foundation, Delaware Valley Regional Planning Commission

Maintenance and Upkeep
Various state, county, and municipal governments, and trail development and volunteer organizations

The Schuylkill Banks Boardwalk is a 2,000-foot-long (610 m) section of the Circuit Trails network that extends roughly 50 feet (15 m) from the Schuylkill Riverbank in Center City, Philadelphia. *(Rails-to-Trails Conservancy)*

THE CIRCUIT is a growing regional trail network that connects destinations across Greater Philadelphia. Consisting of paths that link city centers, transit hubs, parks, and recreational destinations, the Circuit allows pedestrians and bicyclists to travel among urban, suburban, and rural destinations without having to use a motor vehicle.

With 300 miles (483 km) in place and ongoing progress toward the goal of reaching 750 miles (1,200 km) of trails before 2040, the Circuit is emerging as a key component of the overall transportation system in Greater Philadelphia. The real estate community has taken notice. Developers building near the Circuit have noted trail access as a key amenity for residential and commercial properties, and homeowners close to Circuit trails are experiencing increased property values.

Project Background

Bicycling in Philadelphia. The Circuit, Greater Philadelphia's regional trail network, connects towns and cities across the area, providing pedestrians and bicyclists with car-free routes among diverse destinations, including downtown Philadelphia; Camden, New Jersey; and the Valley Forge National Historical Park. Along the way, trail users can access public transportation services, employment centers, open space, and various town centers. At present, 300 miles (483 km) of the network are in place, with a total of 750 miles (1,200 km) planned.

The Circuit expands on over a quarter-century of successful, yet piecemeal, trail development in the region and channels local support for improved active transportation infrastructure.

In 2015, Michael Nutter, former mayor of Philadelphia, summed up the effects of the popularity of bicycling in the city, noting, "Of the top ten big cities of America, Philadelphia has the highest percentage of bicycle commuters per capita. . . . Bicycling is a fundamental aspect of a city's mobility, economic development, public health, and environmental sustainability."

The U.S. Census shows that bicycle commuting in the Philadelphia region increased 151 percent from 2000 to 2009, and in 2014, 1.9 percent of Philadelphia commuters traveled by bike—a rate 1.75 times that of New York City and over three times higher than that of the United States as a whole.

Connecting regional trails. Due in large part to the high rate of bicycling in Philadelphia and the ongoing construction of paths like the Schuylkill River Trail, which sees up to 1 million users annually, leaders from the William Penn Foundation, a private philanthropic organization, and transportation and environmental advocates from the Bicycle Coalition of Greater Philadelphia and the Pennsylvania Environmental Council began to convene those involved with local trail planning, building, and programming in

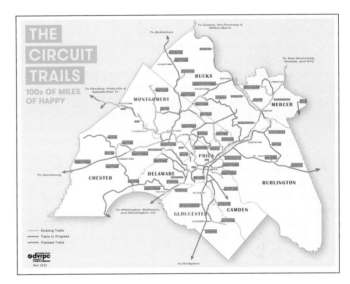

As of 2015, 300 miles (483 km) of the planned 750-mile (1,200 km) Circuit Trails network were in place, with many more in development. *(Delaware Valley Regional Planning Commission)*

2010. This effort led to the formal creation of the Circuit Coalition in 2012, a group tasked with connecting the region's disjointed trails across nine local counties.

The Circuit Coalition includes more than 40 partner organizations, ranging from nonprofit advocacy groups, private foundations, and state, county, and local governments. The coalition engages in a wide array of activities, including advocating for trail funding, managing trail construction projects, and working with private developers and other companies to see trails incorporated into their developments.

Funding for the Circuit comes from a variety of sources. The William Penn Foundation has financed many of the efforts of the Circuit Coalition and has made a significant financial contribution

The Circuit Trails connect pedestrians and bicyclists to local parks, including Cooper River Park in Pennsauken, New Jersey. (Rails-to-Trails Conservancy)

to the planning, design, and construction of individual trail segments. Government transportation funds (federal, state, county, and local) also have funded Circuit trails, while nonprofit groups and donations from area residents and private companies—including real estate development firms with properties on or near the Circuit—have funded trail infrastructure as well.

Since the effort to connect the Circuit was launched, over 50 miles (80 km) of new trails have opened, with many more in development. Over 25 percent of the Philadelphia region lives within one mile (1.6 km) of a completed Circuit trail. Finishing the network will raise that figure to 50 percent.

The Circuit enjoys broad support. A 2015 survey conducted by the Bicycle Coalition of Greater Philadelphia found that 85 percent of area residents supported building more trails in their counties and 60 percent of respondents said they would like to have access to a trail within ten minutes of their homes.

Development, Quality of Life, and Economic Impacts

Investments in the Circuit have led to significant positive economic impacts for developers, local residents, and area municipal governments. When the Circuit was launched in 2012, Mayor Nutter explained how trail development can spur economic activity, stating, "Connecting the Circuit of trails in our region makes the Greater Philadelphia region a stronger, smarter, and more sustainable urban and suburban environment that attracts new companies and employers who choose to base their operations here."

Across the region, the statistics speak for themselves. The Rails-to-Trails Conservancy found that the Schuylkill River Trail, a popular Circuit route, generated $7.3 million in direct economic impact along its route in 2009, and the Delaware & Lehigh Trail, a 165-mile (265 km) rail-trail through eastern Pennsylvania, was found to have generated an annual economic impact exceeding $19 million in 2012. In addition, Rutgers University found that active transportation–related events, businesses, and infrastructure, including the Circuit, were estimated to have contributed $498 million to the New Jersey economy in 2011.

Local residents are benefiting from higher property values along a number of Circuit routes. For example, a 2011 study by the GreenSpace Alliance and the Delaware Valley Regional Planning Commission found that properties within a quarter-mile (0.4 km) of the Radnor Trail, a 2.4-mile (3.9 km) trail in Radnor Township, Pennsylvania, were valued on average $69,000 higher than other area properties further away. Real estate listings in Radnor frequently mention trail access in their advertisements, and for-sale signs often appear on the trail side of properties.

Residential developers have built properties with features that support use of Circuit trails, including the Station at Manayunk, a 149-unit apartment complex on a former brownfield adjacent to the Manayunk Canal Towpath. Developed by J.G. Petrucci, the project was completed in 2014 and features an on-site bike repair shop, a resident bike-share program, and a bicycle wheeling ramp down to the trail, allowing residents to commute by bike to Center City, Philadelphia.

In Philadelphia, Brandywine Realty Trust is developing trail-side properties, including the FMC Tower, a 49-story, 730-foot-tall (222 m) mixed-use skyscraper scheduled to be completed in 2016. Access to the Schuylkill River Trail is touted in advertisements for the tower. Gerard H. Sweeney, Brandywine's president and chief executive officer, expressed his company's support for connecting regional trails in a 2013 letter to the city of Philadelphia, stating, "When fully complete, the Circuit will help connect people to jobs, recreational opportunities, public transportation, and other neighborhoods, and will serve as a gateway to open green space."

Area private companies have invested directly in Circuit trails. Bristol-Myers Squibb, which has a major facility in Lawrenceville, New Jersey, has provided more than $2.5 million for the development and construction of the 22-mile (35 km) Lawrence-Hopewell Trail, a portion of the Circuit close to Princeton, New Jersey. Educational Testing Services, also located along the route, gave additional financial support, and Brandywine Realty Trust built a segment of the Lawrence-Hopewell Trail running through the Princeton Pike Corporate Center at its own expense.

The trails of the Circuit also contribute to the health of Greater Philadelphia. A 2011 study by the GreenSpace Alliance and the Delaware Valley Regional Planning Commission found that residents' use of southeastern Pennsylvania's parks and trails, including the Circuit, avoids $199 million per year in direct medical costs and $596 million in indirect costs.

The continuing success of the Circuit shows how connected trails can have regional benefits beyond recreation. Across Greater Philadelphia, residents are using trails to get to work, to reach public transportation, and to exercise. The Circuit has also increased local property values and encouraged residential and commercial development along its many routes. As the network continues to expand, there will be further opportunities to invest in private development projects that both benefit from and support active transportation assets across the region.

Top: The Schuylkill Banks Boardwalk, part of the Circuit Trails network, allows pedestrians and bicyclists to commute, exercise, or relax over the Schuylkill River in Philadelphia. *(Rails-to-Trails Conservancy)*

Bottom: The Circuit Trails network features a mix of local and regional trails, including the Delaware River Heritage Trail. *(Rails-to-Trails Conservancy)*

Cycle Superhighways
(Supercykelstier)
Copenhagen, Denmark

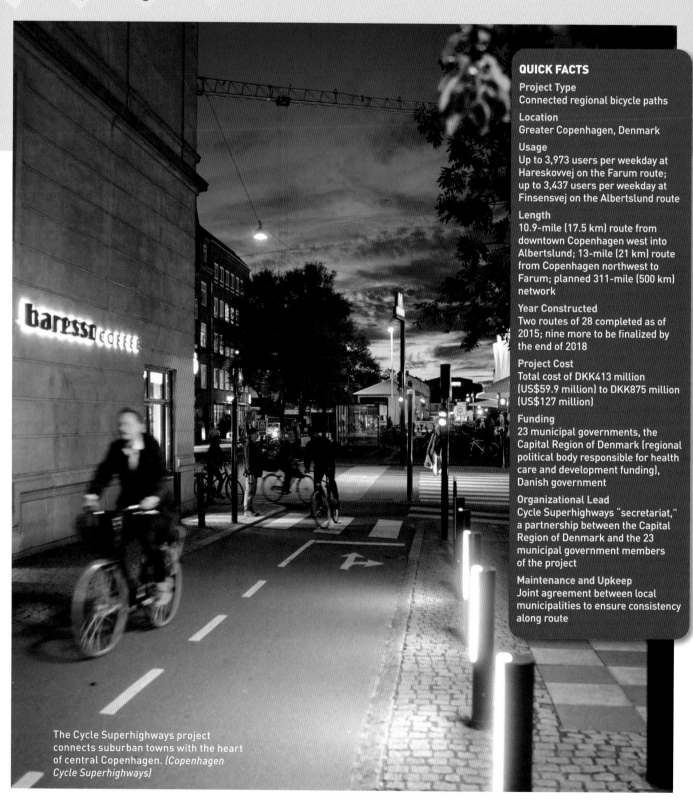

QUICK FACTS

Project Type
Connected regional bicycle paths

Location
Greater Copenhagen, Denmark

Usage
Up to 3,973 users per weekday at Hareskovvej on the Farum route; up to 3,437 users per weekday at Finsensvej on the Albertslund route

Length
10.9-mile (17.5 km) route from downtown Copenhagen west into Albertslund; 13-mile (21 km) route from Copenhagen northwest to Farum; planned 311-mile (500 km) network

Year Constructed
Two routes of 28 completed as of 2015; nine more to be finalized by the end of 2018

Project Cost
Total cost of DKK413 million (US$59.9 million) to DKK875 million (US$127 million)

Funding
23 municipal governments, the Capital Region of Denmark (regional political body responsible for health care and development funding), Danish government

Organizational Lead
Cycle Superhighways "secretariat," a partnership between the Capital Region of Denmark and the 23 municipal government members of the project

Maintenance and Upkeep
Joint agreement between local municipalities to ensure consistency along route

The Cycle Superhighways project connects suburban towns with the heart of central Copenhagen. *(Copenhagen Cycle Superhighways)*

IN 2012, the first of a planned network of 28 "cycle superhighways" opened in Copenhagen, with a second route opening in 2013. These upgraded bike paths connect the central city with suburban areas and link residential neighborhoods, schools, and business districts.

The cycle superhighways were planned to meet the needs of commuters in outlying parts of the Copenhagen region by creating long-distance routes with consistent, high-quality design standards. The project is intended to entice thousands of daily commuters to switch from driving to bicycling, thereby decreasing traffic congestion, carbon emissions, and health care costs, while increasing the quality of life of area residents.

Project Background

Bicycling in Copenhagen. The capital of Denmark has long been recognized as an international hub for bicycle culture due to its commitment to creating safe and efficient cycling infrastructure. According to the Danish government, there are more bikes in Copenhagen than inhabitants and the city boasts nearly 249 miles (400 km) of bike lanes—including the world's busiest. Fifty percent of Copenhagen residents commute to work on a bike daily.

Pia Allerslev, mayor of Copenhagen for children and youth, explains how bicycling is part of daily life in the city, stating, "The bicycle offers a cheap, comfortable, easy, and eco-friendly way of getting around. When we ask Copenhageners why they choose their bike over the car or public transport, they simply answer, 'Because it's the fastest way of getting around in the city.' "

Connecting regional cycle routes. Even though bicycle commuting rates in Copenhagen were already significant, leaders from across the Capital Region came together in 2009 to further improve cycling infrastructure. This effort resulted in a plan to create 28 Cycle Superhighway, or "bike-bahn," routes, by connecting and improving existing bike paths. By 2015, 23 municipalities were working together to develop the cycle superhighways.

Funding for the network comes from local municipalities and the Danish government. The 23 municipalities involved in the project are each responsible for the construction, operation, and maintenance of their portion of the network and pay half of the cost of constructing paths within their borders. The remaining costs are subsidized by the national government. A regional steering committee facilitates the planning work leading to the development of the routes, ensuring consistent design.

When complete, the network will include 311 miles (500 km) of cycle superhighways, at a budget of DKK413 million (US$59.9 million) to DKK875 million (US$127 million), depending on final design decisions.

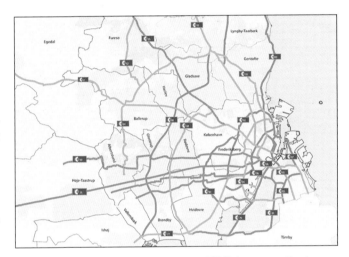

A total of 28 Cycle Superhighway routes will link surrounding towns and neighborhoods with central Copenhagen. *(Copenhagen Cycle Superhighways)*

The underlying goal of the Cycle Superhighway plan is to increase bicycle commuting for those who travel distances exceeding 3.1 miles (5 km) from home to work, with a target of an additional 15,000 people opting to bike to work rather than drive, resulting in a 30 percent increase in bike commuting across the Capital Region.

As of 2015, two of the planned 28 Cycle Superhighway routes were open to the public, with nine more scheduled for completion by 2018. One finished route connects Copenhagen to Albertslund, a suburban community 11 miles (18 km) west of the city. The second links Copenhagen with Farum, a municipality 13 miles (21 km) northwest of Copenhagen. While these routes radiate out from central Copenhagen, future routes will also form links between suburbs.

The completed paths are already reshaping transportation in the region. The Farum Route saw a 52 percent increase in the number of cyclists traveling along the corridor between 2012 and 2014. Among Farum Route commuters, 21 percent were

Top: New uniform signage provides bicyclists using the cycle superhighways with clear routes between suburban towns and central Copenhagen. *(Copenhagen Cycle Superhighways)*

Center: LED lights along the path of the cycle superhighways automatically turn on when cyclists are present. *(Copenhagen Cycle Superhighways)*

Bottom: Many Cycle Superhighway routes are adjacent to roadways, but are physically separated from automobile traffic and pedestrians. *(Copenhagen Cycle Superhighways)*

new to bike commuting and 14 percent said they used the route more often after improvements. Users of the path were also surveyed about safety concerns, ranging from lighting to the potential for collisions, and reported an 11 percent increase in perceived safety due to improvements.

Cycle superhighway design features. The cycle superhighways are being formed by patching together and improving existing cycle routes. The paths feature smooth asphalt surfaces, shelters, and innovative lighting. In some areas, light-emitting diode (LED) lights sense whether cyclists are on the route and automatically turn off when sections are empty, resulting in an 80 percent reduction of power use.

Each superhighway is equipped with a bicycle pump at every mile, as well as foot rests at intersections that prevent cyclists from having to get off bikes when stopped.

Another major innovation is "green wave" technology that times traffic lights to the average bicycling speed of 12 miles (19 km) per hour and provides riders traveling at this speed with continuous green lights.

Cycle superhighways have varying widths, with less heavily traveled routes at 8.2 feet (2.5 m) wide, and busier stretches closer to central Copenhagen at 9.8 to 13.1 feet (3 to 4 m) wide. These widths are standard for the region, yet consistently allow two people to bike side-by-side.

Development, Quality of Life, and Economic Impacts

The city of Copenhagen found in 2010 that, across Denmark, every kilometer traveled by bike earns the country DKK1.22 (US$0.18), while every kilometer traveled by car costs the nation DKK0.69 (US$0.10). Furthermore, the University of Denmark estimates that automobile traffic congestion costs the Capital Region an average of DKK10 billion (US$1.45 billion) per year.

The increase in cycling, and corresponding reduction in automobile use, produced by the opening of the cycle superhighways are expected to further contribute to the economic health of the Copenhagen region. The Capital Region predicts an economic return from the completed network of 19 percent, due to health care savings from increased physical activity, reduced air pollution levels, and fewer road fatalities. This compares favorably with the rate of return the Capital Region sees on investments in roadway projects. For example, Ring 3, a highway encircling Copenhagen, saw a rate of return of just 2.8 percent.

The Capital Region government estimates that the increase in physical activity created by the cycle superhighways will lead to 34,000 fewer sick days per year and a $60 million reduction in health care costs, as well as a decrease of 1.4 million car trips taken per year and an annual reduction in CO_2 emissions equaling 856 tons.

As the Cycle Superhighway network grows, local governments and the private sector are working together to ensure that new residential and commercial developments will be accessible by bicycle. One major initiative is the Nordhavn district, a former port area of Copenhagen that is being redeveloped as a living and working district expected to house 45,000 residents. A new cycle superhighway, along with rail transit service, will be the main forms of transportation in Nordhavn.

The Ørestad area of Copenhagen, an area of the city that has seen continuing large-scale development since the 1990s, is already connected to other parts of the city by rail service and designated bike routes, but there also are plans to further improve connectivity by incorporating the Cycle Superhighway network into the local plan for the area.

Ørestad is already home to bicycle-friendly real estate developments, including the mixed-use 8 Tallet or "Big House," the largest private development ever undertaken in Copenhagen, which is designed with exterior ramps that allow residents on all ten floors of the building to access their front door by bicycle.

The plan for the cycle superhighways builds off Copenhagen's existing network of bike lanes, trails, and other cycle-related infrastructure, which supports bicycle-friendly development projects. The completed Cycle Superhighway routes have already increased the rates of bicycling from suburban areas into central Copenhagen.

The cycle superhighways are an example of municipal coordination that has health and economic benefits for the entire region, further contributing to Copenhagen's role as a vibrant, livable city that is continuing to develop in a sustainable way.

Footrests allow users of the cycle superhighways to stop at red lights without having to get off their bikes. (Copenhagen Cycle Superhighways)

Cycle Superhighways
London, United Kingdom

QUICK FACTS

Project Type
Bicycle lanes, segregated from motor vehicle traffic, called "cycle superhighways"

Location
London, United Kingdom

Usage
East–West Superhighway planned capacity of 3,000 cyclists/hour; North–South Superhighway planned capacity of 2,500 cyclists/hour

Length
East–West Superhighway will be 18 miles (29 km), from Barking to Acton; North–South Superhighway will be three miles (5 km), from King's Cross to Elephant and Castle

Year Constructed
Construction began in the spring of 2015; scheduled to be completed in the summer of 2016

Project Cost
£160 million (US$240 million)

Funding
Public transit fares, London Congestion Charge, government grants, borrowing, and income from advertising and property rental

Organizational Lead
Transport for London

Maintenance and Upkeep
Shared among Transport for London, the 32 London boroughs, and the city of London

A rendering of the East–West Cycle Superhighway along a portion of Victoria Embankment in central London shows the planned separation of bicycles, vehicular traffic, and pedestrians. *(Transport for London)*

IN SPRING 2015, construction began on two cycle superhighways that will connect central London and outlying areas of the capital with bicycling routes that are largely physically segregated from motor vehicle traffic. Also known as "Crossrail for Bikes," a name evoking the east–west commuter rail line that is being built underneath central London, the new cycle routes are meant to be used as alternatives to driving or taking public transportation.

In addition to road safety benefits and an increase in the proportion of bicycle commuters, the £160 million (US$240 million) investment in the creation of the cycle superhighways is spurring new residential and commercial development along the routes.

Project Background

Bicycling in London. The demand for a system of cycle super-highways and the shift to bicycle-friendly development projects are a reflection of the changing landscape of transportation in and around London. Between 2001 and 2011, the number of Londoners who cycled to work more than doubled from 77,000 to 155,000, and bicycles now make up nearly a quarter of vehicles on the road during rush hour in central London. London is also home to more than 700 "Santander Cycles" bike-share stations with over 10,000 bikes available for short-term rentals.

In an effort to cater to existing bike commuters and further expand the number of cyclists in London, Ken Livingstone, the former mayor, and Transport for London, the local governmental body responsible for transportation throughout the region, began working in 2008 to create commuter cycling routes across London, a project that continues under Mayor Boris Johnson.

As of 2015, four cycling routes have been completed, but they have been criticized for their lack of physical separation from motor vehicle traffic. Six bicyclists were killed on the route known as "CS2" between 2011 and 2015.

Creating new cycle superhighways. The two new cycle super-highways scheduled to open in the spring of 2016 differ in that paths and bike lanes will largely be segregated from motor vehicle traffic, helping decrease the likelihood of cyclist injuries and deaths. In addition, CS2 is being reconstructed to improve its safety by providing separated tracks along most of its route.

More than 30 of London's most dangerous intersections will be improved along the two brand-new cycle superhighways routes, with the aim of reducing cyclist fatalities and conflicts with large trucks, which make up only 5 percent of vehicles on the road but cause over 50 percent of all cyclist deaths. There also will be significant benefits to pedestrian safety, because the superhighways will result in more than 16,000 feet (4,900 m) of new sidewalk space and 22 new pedestrian crossings.

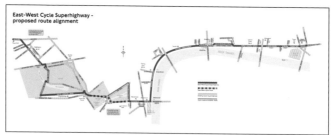

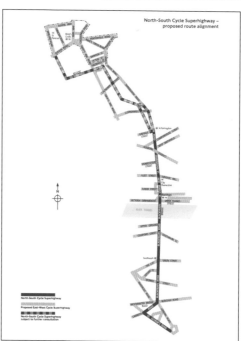

Top: London's 18-mile (29 km) East–West Cycle Superhighway will link Tower Hill to Lancaster Gate. It is scheduled to be completed by summer 2016. *(Transport for London)*

Bottom: London's three-mile (5 km) North–South Cycle Superhighway will link Elephant and Castle to Stonecutter Street, near Holborn Viaduct. It is scheduled to be completed by spring 2016. *(Transport for London)*

Above: Features such as dedicated signals for cyclists at intersections will improve the safety of bicycling around central London. *(Transport for London)*

Right: A cyclist rides along a segregated cycle track on Victoria Embankment in central London. *(Transport for London)*

The cycle superhighways will cost £160 million (US$240 million), with funding coming from Transport for London, whose revenue is generated through a mix of public transit fares, the London Congestion Charge (a fee charged on most motor vehicles entering central London during the day on weekdays), government grants, borrowing, and income from advertising and property rental.

The new cycle superhighways will traverse London 18 miles (29 km) from east to west, between Barking and Acton, and three miles (5 km) north to south, between King's Cross and Elephant and Castle, creating connections among residential areas, transit stations, places of employment, and parks.

Along the cycle superhighway routes, bike riders will pass near landmarks, such as Hyde Park, Buckingham Palace, the Houses of Parliament, and the Tower of London. The first nearly mile-long (1.6 km) section opened in November 2015, with the remaining construction scheduled to be completed by the summer of 2016.

Improved design features of the cycle superhighways will include physical separation from motor vehicle traffic, signalized cycle crossings to allow cyclists to safely cross busy roads, traffic signal changes to allow cyclists to proceed before other traffic, and new LED lighting.

Development, Quality of Life, and Economic Impacts

The increasing popularity of bicycling in London has positive economic implications for the region and the United Kingdom as a whole. The London School of Economics found in 2011 that cycling generates nearly £3 billion (US$4.32 billion) for the U.K. economy each year.

Mayor Johnson has championed the economic and quality-of-life benefits of bicycling and the cycle superhighways, noting that they are an essential part of the city's effort to accommodate residential growth and development. He has said, "With London's population growing by 10,000 a month, there are only two ways to keep traffic moving—build more roads, which is for the most part physically impossible, or encourage the use of vehicles, such as bikes, which better use the space on the roads we've already got."

Building the cycle superhighways is expected to benefit London by reducing traffic congestion. Transport for London estimates that the new east–west bicycle superhighway will be able to accommodate up to 3,000 people an hour, which would be equivalent to adding 41 fully loaded double-decker buses to the route that parallels the superhighway. The north–south route is expected to carry up to 2,500 cyclists an hour, equivalent to

the capacity of 34 extra buses. Given that the routes also largely align with London Underground transit lines, these super-highways are expected to take many commuters off the trains, reducing transit congestion and increasing travel capacity into central London.

Due to the reduced traffic congestion and increased physical activity that the cycle superhighways are expected to produce, Transport for London predicts that improved public health and environmental outcomes will lead to a net £76 million (US$110 million) economic benefit for London over the next 30 years.

The economic benefits of the cycle superhighways also extend to new development projects, since coordination among Transport for London, local governments, and area developers has led to plans for new apartments, offices, shops, restaurants, and bars along the routes.

Examples of developments along the planned cycle super-highways include the following: Elephant Park, a 2,500-unit residential development at the southern end of the north–south route that will include cycle paths that connect to the superhigh-way and 250 City Road, a 930-unit apartment development close to the cycle superhighways, which will include 1,486 bicycle parking spaces (see 250 City Road profile).

The combination of the growing number of commuter cyclists in London and the increasing popularity of bicycle-friendly development projects has significant positive implications for the health, safety, livability, and economy of London.

As the city's population continues to grow, providing safe and convenient bicycle infrastructure can help reduce traffic conges-tion and catalyze new development opportunities that leverage the shift toward active transportation throughout London.

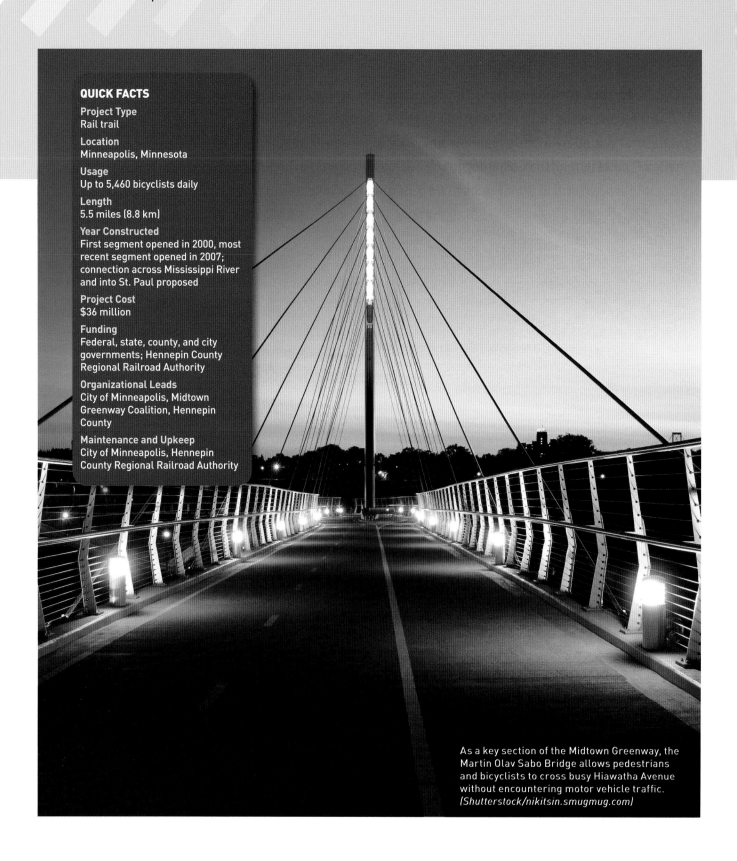

Midtown Greenway
Minneapolis, Minnesota

QUICK FACTS

Project Type
Rail trail

Location
Minneapolis, Minnesota

Usage
Up to 5,460 bicyclists daily

Length
5.5 miles (8.8 km)

Year Constructed
First segment opened in 2000, most recent segment opened in 2007; connection across Mississippi River and into St. Paul proposed

Project Cost
$36 million

Funding
Federal, state, county, and city governments; Hennepin County Regional Railroad Authority

Organizational Leads
City of Minneapolis, Midtown Greenway Coalition, Hennepin County

Maintenance and Upkeep
City of Minneapolis, Hennepin County Regional Railroad Authority

As a key section of the Midtown Greenway, the Martin Olav Sabo Bridge allows pedestrians and bicyclists to cross busy Hiawatha Avenue without encountering motor vehicle traffic. (Shutterstock/nikitsin.smugmug.com)

THE MIDTOWN GREENWAY is a commuter trail in Minneapolis that was built in stages between 2000 and 2007, with future extensions still to come. The Greenway provides healthy and safe automobile traffic–free connections between key destinations in south Minneapolis and facilitates access to the heart of downtown due to its links with other bicycle and pedestrian infrastructure.

The Midtown Greenway has come to be known as a "bicycle freeway" because it includes separate one-way paths for each direction of bicycle travel and a parallel two-way pedestrian path. The creation of the Greenway has led to an explosion of residential and commercial development along the surrounding corridor.

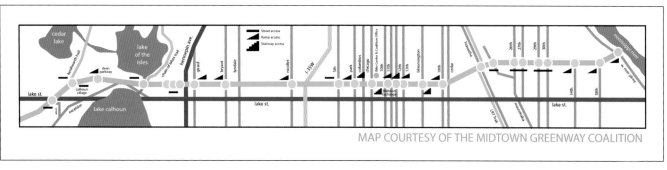

MAP COURTESY OF THE MIDTOWN GREENWAY COALITION

The Midtown Greenway connects popular Minneapolis neighborhoods with parks and open space. *(The Midtown Greenway Coalition)*

Project Background

Bicycling in Minneapolis. With more than 200 miles (322 km) of bikeways, cycling as a means of transportation has become a way of life for many in Minneapolis. Due in part to the completion of the Midtown Greenway, Minneapolis experienced a 76 percent increase in cycling between 2007 and 2013. The city's bike-share system, Nice Ride Minnesota, also supports trail use and includes 170 stations, many located along Minneapolis's bicycle freeways.

Minneapolis Mayor Betsy Hodges explained that active transportation has flourished in her city—despite its harsh winters—because of the emphasis that local leaders have placed on improving conditions for bicyclists. The mayor stated, "Minneapolis has long been recognized as one of the best bicycling cities in the country. . . . We have the second-highest rate of people biking to work among large U.S. cities, including winter commuting. Much of this is possible because of our city's efforts to maintain off-street trails year-round."

The Midtown Greenway—a "bicycle freeway." The Midtown Greenway runs 5.5 miles (8.8 km) east to west along a former rail corridor in south Minneapolis. The trail connects the Uptown neighborhood, the Mississippi River waterfront, the Chain of

Lakes park area, and various bicycling routes, including the Southwest Light-Rail Transit and Hiawatha Trails.

Following the example of Minneapolis's Cedar Lake Trail, which was built between 1995 and 2011 and was the first in the United States to implement the "bicycle freeway" concept of segregated travel lanes, the Midtown Greenway includes two unidirectional paths for bicyclists and a multidirectional path for pedestrians.

Before the first segment of the Midtown Greenway opened in 2000, the freight railway corridor where the Greenway was eventually built had become littered with trash; it had not been operational since the early 1990s. Recognizing the potential of the corridor as an active transportation route, the Midtown Greenway Coalition was formed in 1995 to advocate for the rail-way's transformation into the bicycle freeway that it is today.

Neighborhoods adjacent to the corridor range from Uptown, a long-popular commercial and entertainment district, to industrial areas that had experienced significant disinvestment. Residential neighborhoods of varying densities also line the corridor.

The Midtown Greenway Coalition worked with the city of Minneapolis and other public agencies throughout the process of planning and constructing the Greenway. The coalition continues to engage with local residents, businesses, and private developers to ensure that the Greenway is protected and continually improved.

Funding for the Midtown Greenway came from a variety of sources, including government funds (federal, county, state, city, and neighborhood), the Hennepin County Regional Railroad Authority, and a congressional earmark. Private funds—including from real estate developers—also have been used to improve access to the trail, by way of pedestrian and bicyclist bridges and ramps. Segments of the Midtown Greenway opened in phases beginning in 2000, with the most recent section—the pedestrian- and bicyclist-only Martin Olav Sabo Bridge—coming on line in 2007. The bridge connected two existing sections of the Greenway and eliminated the need for trail users to cross the seven-lane Hiawatha Avenue at street level. At 20 feet (6 m) below grade, the Midtown Greenway is well lit and snow is plowed in the winter less than 24 hours after it falls, making it accessible at all times of the year. Ramps along the Greenway allow users to exit the trail to reach local places of employment, shops, residences, and restaurants.

The Midtown Greenway forms connections to Minneapolis's growing transit and trail network, allowing rail and bus riders to complete their journeys by walking or bicycling. The Hiawatha Trail connects the Greenway to the Lake Street Midtown station on the 12-mile (19 km) Blue Line light-rail service. Trail users can also connect to the Cedar Lake Trail via the Kenilworth Trail to reach downtown and Target Field Station, a major transit hub, and the meeting point of two light-rail lines, heavy-rail commuter service, and numerous bus routes.

The Midtown Greenway includes separate lanes for opposing directions of bicycle traffic, as well as dedicated space for pedestrians. *(Tim Springer)*

Development, Quality of Life, and Economic Impacts

The Midtown Greenway has transformed commuting options and improved the quality of life in many Minneapolis neighborhoods, and the real estate community has taken note.

Along the Midtown Greenway route, at least 11 separate projects, ten of which are residential, were developed between 2004 and 2014. According to Hennepin County Commissioner Peter McLaughlin, property values along the corridor have increased by over 90 percent in the past ten years.

The Midtown Greenway Coalition is strongly in support of development along the trail and frequently provides feedback to developers to make sure that project designs help ensure the continued success of the Greenway. Soren Jensen, the coalition's executive director, explains, "The Midtown Greenway has helped spark more than $750 million worth of new housing developments along its edges. It has truly helped to revitalize south Minneapolis, as well as helping to spark the biking renaissance in Minneapolis."

Highlights of the numerous recent projects developed along the Midtown Greenway include the following:

>> **The Midtown Exchange,** a $190 million project that redeveloped a formerly abandoned Sears distribution center, which is the second-largest building in Minnesota in terms of leasable space. Completed in 2006, the 1.2 million-square-foot (111,500 sq m) development included a mix of office, residential, hotel, and retail space, with multiple access points and entrances along the Midtown Greenway.

>> **Elan Uptown,** a 591-unit, $150 million residential development built in 2013 that includes a three-block public promenade along the Greenway and direct trail access for residents.

>> **Track 29 City Apartments,** a 198-unit, $38.5 million residential development that includes a ramp and public promenade for Midtown Greenway users, as well as bike storage and a bicycle repair facility.

>> **Lime,** a $36.5 million mixed-use project with 171 apartments and 8,500 square feet (800 sq m) of retail space. The Midtown Greenway Coalition worked with project developers to ensure that the building did not create shadows that would lead to icing on the Midtown Greenway in winter.

>> **Greenway Heights,** a $9.1 million, 42-unit affordable housing complex with two-, three-, and four-bedroom family apartments built directly adjacent to the Midtown Greenway.

>> **MoZaic,** a $45 million, 77,000-square-foot office (7,200 sq m) and retail development along the Midtown Greenway that includes a ramp and pedestrian bridge that connects to the trail. A second phase of the project is in development (more information on page 26).

Users of the Midtown Greenway in Minneapolis can connect directly to residential areas, offices, and entertainment districts on foot or by bicycle. *(Micah Taylor)*

The development of the Midtown Greenway offers lessons for other cities in how urban trails can form a crucial component of a region's transportation network. The Greenway has attracted residential, office, and retail development along its corridor, and developers have found that prospective tenants see trails as an attractive asset that sets their projects apart from others in the region.

With higher property values along trail corridors and the continuing expansion of bicycle infrastructure, Minneapolis is illustrating the role that bicycle freeways can play in revitalizing once-underused corridors in a healthy and economically beneficial way.

Bicycle Sharing
Paris, France; Montreal, Canada; Hangzhou, China

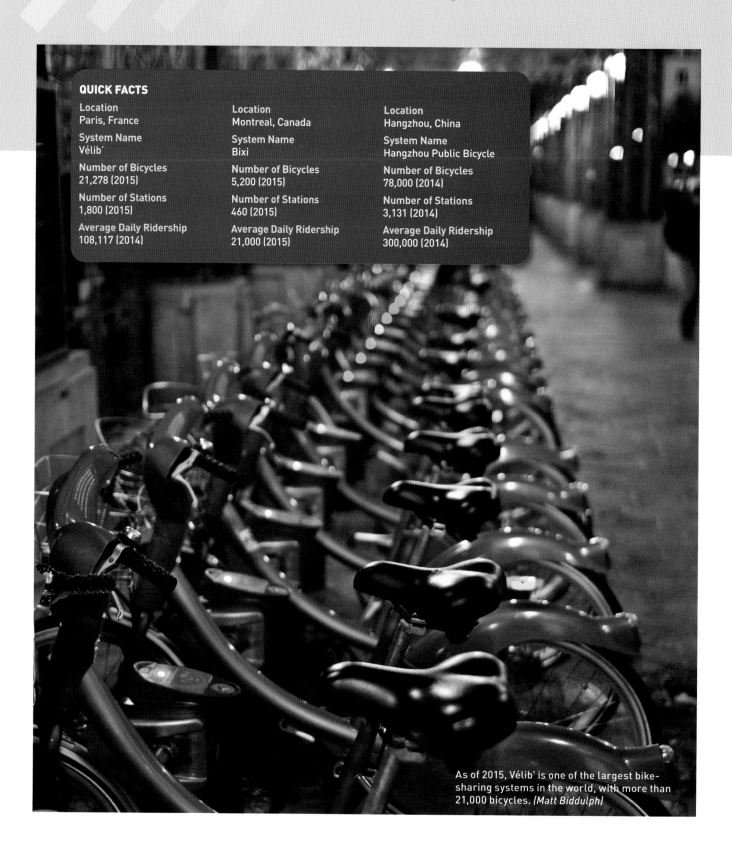

QUICK FACTS

Location Paris, France	**Location** Montreal, Canada	**Location** Hangzhou, China
System Name Vélib'	**System Name** Bixi	**System Name** Hangzhou Public Bicycle
Number of Bicycles 21,278 (2015)	**Number of Bicycles** 5,200 (2015)	**Number of Bicycles** 78,000 (2014)
Number of Stations 1,800 (2015)	**Number of Stations** 460 (2015)	**Number of Stations** 3,131 (2014)
Average Daily Ridership 108,117 (2014)	**Average Daily Ridership** 21,000 (2015)	**Average Daily Ridership** 300,000 (2014)

As of 2015, Vélib' is one of the largest bike-sharing systems in the world, with more than 21,000 bicycles. *(Matt Biddulph)*

BICYCLE-SHARING SYSTEMS—services that allow people to rent or borrow bikes for relatively short durations—have become increasingly popular since the early 2000s in cities throughout the world. In 2004, there were just 13 large municipal bike-share systems worldwide. This figure increased to more than 800 as of 2015—with over 200 in China alone.

By providing low-cost rides, bike-share systems allow riders to commute to work, run errands, or access recreational destinations in a healthy way. Many systems fill in gaps in bus and rail transit networks and have also led to positive economic, health, and development outcomes.

The Evolution of Bike Sharing

The concept of bike sharing on a municipal level was introduced in the 1960s when so-called *witte fietsen*—white bikes—were placed around Amsterdam for use by the public. The idea was that anyone would be able to borrow a bicycle, ride it to his or her destination, and then leave it at that location for someone else to use. However, within a few days, the witte fietsen were largely stolen or vandalized.

A small number of systems that were variations on the witte fietsen concept were attempted over the next 30 years, but most suffered similar issues with theft and maintenance.

The first major innovations to the bike-sharing concept in a large city occurred in 1995, when Copenhagen's *Bycyklen*, or "City Bikes," system was launched. City Bikes, which were built to be more durable than standard bicycles, were placed at 110 locations throughout the central city and could be checked out with a coin deposit for unlimited use.

Features of Modern Bike-Sharing Systems

Various innovations on Copenhagen's City Bikes concept occurred over the next decade, leading to the types of systems frequently seen in the 800-plus cities where bike sharing exists today.

While slight differences exist in the scale and technology used in various bike-sharing systems around the world, most have a few components in common. According to the Institute for Transportation & Development Policy, these features include the following:

>> **Fixed station locations at regular intervals throughout urban areas.** Bike-share stations are generally placed close to areas that generate a significant number of short trips throughout the day, including business districts with large numbers of office workers, areas with a high density of shops and restaurants, tourist destinations, major parks, large residential developments, and transit stations.

>> **Proximity to active transportation infrastructure.** Stations are frequently located along streets with bike lanes, designated bike routes, and commuter trails.

>> **Automated stations.** While some systems are staffed by attendants, the majority of large municipal and regional systems feature automated bicycle docks. Some larger stations are walled, with access through turnstiles instead of having individual docks.

>> **Information technology payment and station locator systems.** Bike-share users rely on smartphone apps, credit cards, and other information technology services to locate bike-share stations and to pay for bike rentals. Charges often increase the longer bikes are checked out to keep bicycles in circulation and to encourage short-distance trips. Many systems offer free 30-minute rides with membership plans.

>> **Durable bikes with standard designs.** Bicycles are built to be sturdy and require minimal maintenance.

>> **Marketing and branding.** Systems have consistent branding and feature distinctive logos and bike designs to set them apart from other transportation modes. Marketing campaigns inform the public about how systems work and how they are integrated with other modes of transportation.

Development, Quality of Life, and Economic Impacts

Bike-sharing programs have a host of benefits for cities and their residents. According to the National League of Cities, benefits include the following: providing low-cost transit options for users in a cost-effective way, reducing traffic congestion, improving access to jobs, increasing retail exposure and home values, increasing overall levels of physical activity, and decreasing levels of air pollution.

The Vélib' bike-share system in Paris features stations located across the city and surrounding municipalities. *(David McSpadden)*

Paris Vélib': A Scaled-Up System of Bike Sharing

In 2007, Paris launched the Vélib' bike-sharing program with 7,000 bikes. By 2008, municipal data showed a 70 percent increase in bike riding and a 5 percent reduction in car use. As of 2013, Vélib' had the highest market penetration of any bike-sharing system in the world, with one bike per 97 residents. By 2015, the number of available bikes had more than tripled, with 21,278 bicycles spread across over 1,800 docking stations throughout the city.

Vélib' is financed and run by the French advertising firm JCDecaux. In an agreement with the city of Paris, JCDecaux was given the right to install advertisements in locations throughout the city, keeping associated profits, while the income generated by Vélib' user fees—estimated at €30 million (US$32.49 million) annually—goes to the city's general budget. Vélib' is the world's longest-running public/private partnership bike-sharing system.

Shortly after Vélib' began service, Bertrand Delanoë, then mayor of Paris, explained his support for the program by noting that "Vélib' is a high-performance service that enables everyone to take advantage of a practical, inexpensive, and ecological means of transport 24 hours a day and seven days a week, providing a new approach to urban mobility."

The scale and success of Vélib' inspired the creation of bike-share systems throughout the world.

Montreal Bixi: Bike Sharing and Increased Property Values

The city of Montreal started a municipally run bike-share system in 2009, called Bixi. It was modeled after Paris's Vélib' and was the first bike-sharing system in North America. By 2015, the Bixi system included 5,200 bikes across 460 stations.

While the system has experienced financial difficulties, including declaring bankruptcy in 2014, it remains popular with Montreal residents and accommodated 3.5 million rides in 2015, an increase of 9.4 percent from the previous year.

Canadian businessman Bruno Rodi, who financed a bailout of the system in 2014, explains the importance of the system to Montreal, saying, "Bixi is part of the signature of Montreal. It symbolizes an active city, a clean city, modern, and focused on sustainable development." Today, Bixi is run by the nonprofit organization Bixi Montreal, with funding from user fees and the city of Montreal.

Bixi has had positive economic impacts for Montreal. According to a McGill University study, neighborhoods with 12 stations within a half-mile (800 m) area saw increased property values for multifamily housing units of 2.7 percent.

The study looked at Montreal housing units that were sold multiple times between 1996 and 2012 and found that each single Bixi station within a half-mile (800 m) area increased a unit's value by CA$709 (US$502). Homes in Bixi's coverage area were found to have an average of 12.2 stations within a half-mile (800 m), leading to a CA$8,650 (US$6,123) increase in their values.

With 5,200 bikes across 460 stations as of 2015, Montreal's Bixi bike-share program was the first in North America. *(pdinnen)*

Hangzhou, China: Bicycle Sharing on a Grand Scale

Hangzhou, China's bike-sharing system, Hangzhou Public Bicycle, debuted in 2008 and was the first bike-share program in Mainland China that operated with an information technology–based system. As of 2015, Hangzhou Public Bicycle had 78,000 bikes and 3,131 stations, making it second only to Wuhan, China, in its scope. Funding comes from advertising revenue, user fees, and government subsidies.

Hangzhou's bike-sharing system allows riders to use payment cards for bicycle rentals that can also be used for public transit and taxi services. Bike-share stations are integrated with public transportation routes, with many stations accommodating up to 140 bikes. By 2011, more than 30 percent of Hangzhou commuters used bike sharing as part of their commute.

Due to rapid economic development and significant population growth, Hangzhou—a city with a population of nearly 8.5 million in 2010—is continuing to invest in bike sharing to improve urban mobility. The city has plans to increase the number of bikes in its system to 175,000 by 2020.

As of 2015, the Hangzhou Public Bicycle system had 78,000 bikes and 3,131 stations. *(Payton Chung)*

Bike sharing has been shown to produce positive impacts for the retail sector. A University of California, Berkeley, study found that four out of ten people in Toronto and Montreal shopped more at locations near bike-share stations, while Washington, D.C.'s Capital Bikeshare program found that 82 percent of people were "somewhat more likely" or "much more likely" to patronize a business, restaurant, or shop if it was accessible through a bike-share program.

In a number of instances, cities are working with private businesses and real estate developers to share both the costs and benefits of bike sharing, including in London, where developers of a mixed-use project called 250 City Road are working with the municipal government to finance the creation of a new "Santander Cycles" station on their property (see project profile).

Bike sharing can also contribute to public health. A study by Spain's Centre for Research in Environmental Epidemiology found that Barcelona's bike-share system contributes to reducing yearly CO_2 emissions by an estimated 9,900 tons (9,000 metric tons) and leads to the equivalent of 12 lives saved each year due to increased physical activity, even when controlling for risks of collisions and air pollution.

The benefits of bike sharing for cities and their residents have spurred continuing increases in the number and size of systems. By enhancing the ease of access to active transportation opportunities, bike sharing is shaping transportation planning and real estate development decisions around the world.

Resources

Active Living Research
http://activelivingresearch.org

Alliance for Walking & Biking
www.bikewalkalliance.org

The Circuit Trails
www.connectthecircuit.org

Colorado Health Foundation
www.coloradohealth.org

Cycle Superhighways—Transport for London
https://tfl.gov.uk/modes/cycling/routes-and-maps/cycle-superhighways

Every Body Walk!
http://everybodywalk.org

League of American Bicyclists
www.bikeleague.org

Lloyd EcoDistrict
www.ecolloyd.org

Midtown Greenway Coalition
http://midtowngreenway.org

Nashville Area MPO—Health and Well-Being
www.nashvillempo.org/regional_plan/health

Partnership for Active Transportation
www.railstotrails.org/partnership-for-active-transportation

PeopleForBikes
www.peopleforbikes.org

Project for Public Spaces
www.pps.org

Rails-to-Trails Conservancy
www.railstotrails.org

Robert Wood Johnson Foundation—Designing for Public Health
www.rwjf.org/en/library/research/2005/02/designing-for-active-transportation.html

Smart Growth America
www.smartgrowthamerica.org

Supercykelstier—Copenhagen Cycle Superhighways
www.supercykelstier.dk

Acknowledgments

The Building Healthy Places Initiative gratefully acknowledges the contributions of the following people to this report:

Stuart Ackerberg
Chief Executive Officer
The Ackerberg Group

Chris Abel
Development Director
Berkeley Group

Matt M. Bronfman
Chief Executive Officer
Jamestown

Emily Cohen
Vice President, Marketing and Public Relations
Gotham Organization

Jake D. Dietrich
Director of Development
Milhaus Ventures

Kelsey Gregory
Asset Manager
The Ackerberg Group

Alexander Grgurich
Development Analyst
Nelson Construction & Development

Line Kildegaard Groot
Kommunikation
Supercykelstier

Christopher Jaskiewicz
Chief Operating Officer
Gotham Organization

Soren Jensen
Executive Director
Midtown Greenway Coalition

Wade W. Lange
Vice President, Regional Manager, Portland
American Assets Trust

Chris Linn
Manager, Office of Environmental Planning
Delaware Valley Regional Planning Commission

Jessie Lucero
Property Manager
Silver Moon Lodge Apartments

Jane G. Mahaffie
Principal
StonebridgeCarras

Kelley McLaughlin
Senior Public Relations Manager
Phase:3 Marketing and Communications

Tadd Miller
President and Chief Executive Officer
Milhaus Ventures

Mike Nelson
President and Owner
Nelson Construction & Development

Anna Nørreby
Studentermedhjælper
Sekretariat for Supercykelstier

Tim Springer
The Greenway Guy

Patrick Starr
Executive Vice President for Programs
Pennsylvania Environmental Council

Sarah Clark Stuart
Executive Director
Bicycle Coalition of Greater Philadelphia